The Southwest Economy in the 1990s: A Different Decade

The Southwest Economy in the 1990s:
A Different Decade

Proceedings of the 1989 Conference on the Southwest Economy
Sponsored by the Federal Reserve Bank of Dallas

edited by
Gerald P. O'Driscoll, Jr.
Stephen P.A. Brown
The Federal Reserve Bank of Dallas

Kluwer Academic Publishers
Boston   Dordrecht   London

Distributors for North America:
Kluwer Academic Publishers
101 Philip Drive
Assinippi Park
Norwell, Massachusetts 02061 USA

Distributors for all other countries:
Kluwer Academic Publishers Group
Distribution Centre
Post Office Box 322
3300 AH Dordrecht, THE NETHERLANDS

Library of Congress Cataloging-in-Publication Data

Conference on the Southwest Economy (1989 : Dallas, Tex.)
    The Southwest economy in the 1990s : a different decade : proceedings of
the 1989 Conference on the Southwest Economy / sponsored by the Federal
Reserve Bank of Dallas ; edited by Gerald P. O'Driscoll, Jr., Stephen P.A.
Brown.
      p.   cm.
    Includes bibliographical references.
    ISBN 0-7923-9092-X
    1. Economic forecasting—Southwestern States—Congresses.
2. Southwestern States—Economic conditions—Congresses.
3. Southwestern States—Economic policy—Congresses.
I. O'Driscoll, Gerald P. II. Brown, Stephen P. A. (Stephen Paul
Adolph) 1948—   III. Federal Reserve Bank of Dallas. IV. Title.
HC107.A165C66 1989
330.976'001'12—dc20   90-5349

Contents

Introduction

Overview—The 1990s: A Different Decade ....**xi**

About the Contributors .... **xv**

General Meetings—The 1990s: A Different Decade

Welcome Address—The 1990s: A Different Decade 3
   Robert H. Boykin

The Future of the Southwest Economy: Challenges and Opportunities 5
   Admiral Bobby R. Inman

Research and Public Service in Comprehensive Universities 13
   William H. Cunningham

From Outlook to Opportunity: Making the 1990s Work 19
   John B. McCoy

Session One—Meeting the Challenges in Education

Introductory Remarks—Meeting the Challenges in Education 29
   William H. Wallace

The Case for Educational Choice 31
   John E. Chubb

Schools in the 1990s: The Opportunities and Risks
Facing Texas and Other States 39
    Eric A. Hanushek

American Education After A Nation at Risk 45
    Milton Goldberg

Meeting the Challenges in Education 51
    Paul F. Roth

Session Two—The Challenges of the International Marketplace

The Canada–U.S. Free Trade Agreement:
A New Reality, A New Challenge 57
    Carl E. Rufelds

The Mexican Economy 65
    William C. Gruben

The Challenges of the International Marketplace: The Far East 75
    Lawrence B. Krause

Session Three—Critical Issues

The Role of Financial Institutions in Economic Development 81
    Jerry L. Jordan

Technological Innovation in the Southwest 93
    Keren Ware

The Environment and Economic Growth in the Southwest 99
    John A. Baden

Energy in the Future of the Southwest 121
    Stephen P.A. Brown

Session Four—The Southwest Economy: The Next Year and the Next Decade

Arizona's Economic Outlook 127
   Lee R. McPheters

Louisiana in the 1990s: A Different Decade 139
   Loren C. Scott

The New Mexico Economy 147
   M. Brian McDonald

The Oklahoma Economy: The Next Year and the Next Decade 163
   Larkin Warner

Regional Economic Cycles and the Texas Economy 181
   Barton A. Smith

Preface

T he 1980s began during a great upswing in the Southwest economy, but
what lay ahead was a decade of plummeting oil prices, deflated real
estate values and unprecedented bank failures. The theme of the Federal
Reserve Bank of Dallas' second annual conference on the Southwest economy,
"The 1990s: A Different Decade," reflected our belief that the beginning of the
new decade would mark a turn toward economic strength in the Southwest.

The conference, held Oct. 26–27, 1989, at Loews Anatole Hotel in Dallas,
Texas, brought together more than 250 interested individuals and speakers for
an exchange of information and ideas. Topics ranged from the current condition
of the Southwest economy to the factors shaping the future.

The influences on the Southwest economy are diverse but interrelated. For
example, the Southwest faces a complex dilemma in reforming its educational
system. As conference speakers illustrated many times, education reform and
the quality of our schools are closely linked to the region's, if not the nation's,
ability to compete in future world markets.

These proceedings follow the basic organizational pattern of the confer-
ence. Keynote and luncheon addresses appear in the first section, General
Meetings—The 1990s: A Different Decade, which includes speeches by Bobby
R. Inman, admiral, United States Navy (retired), and private investor; Robert H.
Boykin, president and chief executive officer of the Federal Reserve Bank of
Dallas; William H. Cunningham, president of the University of Texas, Austin; and
John B. McCoy, chairman and chief executive officer of Banc One Corp.

Session One, Meeting the Challenges in Education, provides insight from
five experts, who survey the current state of education, past attempts at reform
and possible solutions for problems in the educational systems of the Southwest.

Speakers in Session Two, The Challenges of the International Marketplace,
examine U.S. trade relations with two neighboring countries, Canada and
Mexico, and emerging markets in the Far East.

In Session Three, Critical Issues, speakers provide new insight on four topics that have influenced and will continue to influence the region's economic health: finance, energy, technological innovation and the environment.

Session Four, The Southwest Economy: The Next Year and the Next Decade, presents a state-by-state forecast for the Southwest, including Arizona, Louisiana, New Mexico, Oklahoma and Texas.

This conference would not have been possible without the efforts of many people. We wish to thank Lea Anderson, Tara Barrett, Susan August Brown, Britt David, Kim Ernst, Harvey Rosenblum, Paula Tucker, Sammie Vaught and the speakers, who helped make the conference a success.

We also would like to thank our editorial staff, Rhonda Harris, Diana Palmer and Virginia Rogers, who helped make this volume possible.

Gerald P. O'Driscoll, Jr.
Stephen P.A. Brown

Overview—The 1990s: A Different Decade

Sally Bell

I n a simplistic sense, it is obvious that the 1990s will be a different decade. Time, after all, flows smoothly from Dec. 31, 1989, to Jan. 1, 1990, with the gentle tick of a clock. But few would question that the 1990s truly will be different from the 1980s in very fundamental ways—some good, some bad, but most still up for grabs based on the collective decisions we make now.

The Southwest enters the new decade uncertain after many heady years in which business leaders seemingly could not make a wrong decision. Nationally, education is in a shambles. The nation can no longer smugly rely on uncontested dominance economically or politically. We wonder whether we can compete with the Pacific Rim nations, and we shake our heads in simple astonishment as Eastern Europe moves to rejoin the Western world. Many worry that the environment sustaining us may have been so abused that it will turn renegade— in which case, our other worries will not matter.

But the coming decade holds unparalleled opportunities as well, if we are thoughtful enough to discern them and bold enough to seize them. The 1990s, after all, are the early dawn of the second millennium. The Southwest is slowly recovering, sprouting the seeds of new industries that hold the potential for transforming our economy even as traditional bedrock industries erode. Business is realizing that its societal role goes beyond making money; if it wants to lead the way to a prosperous decade, business must be in the forefront of decisions made now in education, environmental policy and a restructured economy. The problems of the 1990s are apparent. It is up to us to shape their solutions to our liking.

Such was the theme of the Second Annual Conference on the Southwest Economy, Oct. 26–27, 1989, sponsored by the Federal Reserve Bank of Dallas. Experts on education, international trade, finance, the environment, energy and individual state economies addressed a capacity audience of business leaders at Dallas' Loews Anatole Hotel.

Robert H. Boykin, president and chief executive officer of the Dallas Fed, wasted no time in presenting the Southwest's challenge. Most of the region is slowly recovering from the debacle of recent years, he said, and it is well-situated for growth in the 1990s if it repositions itself now to capitalize on the opportunities ahead.

Although the region's problems seem diverse, they all are related, Boykin said. The region must revamp the educational system to produce a well-educated work force if it is to have any chance of competing internationally. Yet success in a global economy undergirds the economic strength of each state, which ultimately forms the base to pay for educational reforms. The region's launch into new arenas cannot be made without bold moves from a banking industry now timid after the buffeting of recent years.

In his conference kickoff address, Bobby R. Inman struck the same notes in greater detail, urging Southwest leaders to explore solutions to the problems "before, rather than after, these problems overwhelm us." Inman, a private investor, is a former director of the National Security Agency and founding chairman of Austin's Microelectronics and Computer Technology Corp.

Inman said the region must develop all segments of its economy simultaneously if it hopes to achieve rising living standards for today's children. Facing the necessity of dealing with a unified marketplace in the future, the region cannot depend on its old standby resources of cotton, cattle and energy for its prosperity, he said. Nor can it rely on the burgeoning service industries to boost the quality of life because service jobs typically pay significantly less than the manufacturing jobs they replace.

Ensuing sessions produced similar points. The nation cannot remain competitive unless its educational system can produce skilled workers to match those of other nations, said speakers in a session on educational challenges. Speakers who addressed critical issues for the Southwest said the region may find prosperity again in the 1990s if it summons the courage to make basic changes in the economy. In the ashes of today's bankrupt financial institutions lies the possibility of a reinvigorated industry with the knowledge and insight to recognize the innovations that will create tomorrow's jobs, said Keren Ware, director of the Texas Department of Commerce's Office of Advanced Technology. Indeed, the 1990s can become the "most prosperous decade of the century" if the basic challenges are met successfully, said Jerry L. Jordan, senior vice president and chief economist for First Interstate Bancorp of Los Angeles.

Political uncertainties in the Soviet Union, Eastern Europe and China make a solid and diverse economy at home more important as we enter the new decade, Inman said. He noted that it is too early to know where the extraordinary changes of recent months will lead, so pessimists who think this is "the edge of chaos" with renewed repression to follow could yet be right.

But if massive world peace does indeed break out on the eve of the millennium, fewer weapons will be needed, meaning hardship for the South-western cities whose local economies and employment are buttressed by defense contracts. Only a diverse economy can withstand shocks in a major sector.

Speakers posed similar solutions to the challenges of the 1990s. Perhaps most important, the country needs a skilled and motivated work force because "education is the front line" of anything the nation tries to do. The Southwest must come to grips with its changing demographics that mean more than half of new workers in Texas, New Mexico and Arizona will be minorities by the mid-1990s. Schools that now are not reaching them must find ways to boost performance, or the region will not have the educated work force to solve its other problems.

The Southwest also needs reliable capital sources at reasonable rates to compete globally. It must have a strong research base for the scientific discoveries of the future, but equally important, it must develop the commitment to transform dazzling ideas into useful products. Those products must be the best quality anywhere if we are to persuade the American consumer and the world to buy them.

It is clear that for the new decade there are no shortages of challenges, many of which are strikingly different than those that tested leaders at the beginning of the 1980s. Some problems may seem unsolvable today, but the speakers emphasized that the missing elements are *will* and *imagination*—the use of which are entirely up to us.

Sally Bell is a Dallas-based free-lance writer.

About the Contributors

JOHN A. BADEN is chairman of the Foundation for Research on Economics and the Environment, which he established in 1986. He received his doctorate in government from Indiana University and began his career teaching political science and economics at Montana State University. Baden became director of the Environmental Studies Program at Utah State University, where he was a tenured associate professor of political science and forestry, but he later returned to Montana State University to establish the Center for Political Economy and Natural Resources. He also founded the Political Economy Research Center and was its chairman of the board and president until 1985, when he moved to Dallas to head the Maguire Oil and Gas Institute in the Cox School of Business at Southern Methodist University.

ROBERT H. BOYKIN is president and chief executive officer of the Federal Reserve Bank of Dallas. A native of West Texas, he has a bachelor's degree in business administration and a doctoral degree in law from the University of Texas at Austin and is a graduate of the School of Banking of the South at Louisiana State University. He serves as a member of the Advisory Council for the School of Management and Administration for the University of Texas at Dallas as well as an advisory member of the Dallas Citizens Council. Boykin joined the Dallas Fed as an attorney in 1953. Before his election to president, he served as first vice president and chief operating officer. In his capacity as president of the Dallas Fed, he serves on a rotating basis on the Federal Open Market Committee, which formulates the nation's monetary policy.

STEPHEN P.A. BROWN, assistant vice president and senior economist at the Federal Reserve Bank of Dallas, manages the regional economics section of the Dallas Fed's Research Department. He is the author of numerous articles on business conditions and economic policy. His research, which focuses on energy issues and the Southwest economy, has received international attention from the academic community and media, including such publications as the *New York Times* and *Business Week*. He holds a bachelor's degree in economics from California Polytechnic State College and a master's degree and doctorate in economics from the University of Maryland. Brown joined the Dallas Fed in 1981 after working as an energy economist for Brookhaven National Laboratory and teaching economics at several universities.

JOHN E. CHUBB has been a senior fellow with the Governmental Studies Program at the Brookings Institution since 1984. His areas of expertise include American politics and public policy, with a concentration in education and energy. Before joining Brookings, Chubb was an assistant professor of political science and the associate director of public policy at Stanford University. In 1988, in addition to his work at Brookings, he served as a visiting professor of political science at Johns Hopkins University. He is the author of several books. The most recent is titled, *Can the Government Govern?*

W. MICHAEL COX, who chaired Session Two—The Challenges of the International Marketplace, is vice president and economic advisor at the Federal Reserve Bank of Dallas. His responsibilities include serving the Bank's president as advisor on monetary policy, writing for the Bank's economic publications and making frequent appearances as a public speaker. His research centers on domestic monetary policy, international finance and government debt and deficits. Some of his most widely recognized work focuses on a comprehensive index of the international value of the dollar. Cox received his undergraduate degree in business and economics from Hendrix College and his doctorate in economics from Tulane University. In addition to his role at the Dallas Fed, he is an adjunct professor in the Department of Economics at Southern Methodist University.

WILLIAM H. CUNNINGHAM became the 23rd president of the University of Texas at Austin in 1985. He holds the Regents Chair in Higher Education Leadership and the James L. Bayless Chair for Free Enterprise and is a professor of marketing. Before becoming president of the university, he served as dean of the College and Graduate School of Business Administration. Cunningham is a nationally known marketing scholar and former editor of the *Journal of Marketing*. His research interests include marketing management and research and strategic market planning. He is an author, an instructor and the recipient of several teaching awards from the University of Texas. He received his bachelor's degree, master's degree in business administration and doctorate from Michigan State University and was named a distinguished alumnus of that university in 1983.

MILTON GOLDBERG, director of the Office of Research for the U.S. Department of Education, oversees the work of 20 university-based National Research and Development Centers now researching specific classroom subjects. Goldberg has also served as the executive director for the National Commission on Excellence in Education, which produced the landmark report, *A Nation at Risk*. He has taught students ranging from elementary school through college levels and has written extensively about improving educational quality. He received his bachelor's, master's and doctoral degrees from Temple University.

WILLIAM C. GRUBEN serves as senior economist at the Federal Reserve Bank of Dallas, where his work includes the analysis of U.S.–Mexican economic relations. He holds a doctorate in economics from the University of Texas at Austin and is an adjunct professor of economics at Southern Methodist University. Before joining the Dallas Fed, he was a staff economist at InterFirst Corp. He is a member of *The Dallas Morning News* Board of Economists and the *Kiplinger Texas Letter* Board of Economists. He also serves on the Board of Advisers of the University of Texas Bureau of Business Research.

ERIC A. HANUSHEK chairs the department of economics at the University of Rochester, where he has been a professor of economics and political science since 1978. He was director of Rochester's Public Policy Analysis Program between 1978 and 1983, and from the end of 1983 through 1985, he served as a deputy director of the Congressional Budget Office. He has held academic positions with the U.S. Air Force Academy and Yale University, and he was a senior staff economist at the Council of Economic Advisers. Hanushek is a distinguished graduate of the U.S. Air Force Academy, where he received his bachelor's degree. He received his doctorate in economics from the Massachusetts Institute of Technology.

BOBBY R. INMAN, admiral, United States Navy (retired), and a private investor, previously served as chairman and chief executive officer of Microelectronics and Computer Technology Corp. (MCC) in Austin, Texas. His career with naval intelligence spanned two decades; he retired with the permanent rank of admiral in 1982. Between 1974 and 1982, Inman was director of naval intelligence, director of the National Security Agency and deputy director of the Central Intelligence Agency.

JERRY L. JORDAN is senior vice president and chief economist for First Interstate Bancorp in Los Angeles. He previously was dean of the Anderson School of Management in Albuquerque, N.M., but he took time off from that post to serve as a member of former President Ronald Reagan's Council of Economic Advisers and the U.S. Gold Commission. Jordan holds a Ph.D. in economics from the University of California at Los Angeles. His numerous professional affiliations include membership on the board of directors of the National Association of Business Economists, of which he is a past president.

LAWRENCE B. KRAUSE, a professor in the Graduate School of International Relations and Pacific Studies at the University of California at San Diego, is an expert on trade and economic activity in the Pacific Rim countries. A native of Michigan, he received his bachelor's and master's degrees from the University of Michigan and his doctorate from Harvard University. His experience includes serving as a professor at Yale University and working for the U.S. Department of State, the Council of Economic Advisers and the Brookings Institution. In 1988, he was named coordinator of the Pacific Economic Outlook Project for the Pacific Economic Cooperation Conference. He is the author of numerous articles and books about the Pacific Rim economy.

JOHN B. McCOY is chairman and chief executive officer of Banc One Corporation. McCoy, a Banc One associate since 1970, served as president of Bank One, Columbus (Ohio), before becoming president—and later chairman—of the Banc One holding company. McCoy is very active in community affairs and serves on the boards of the Columbus Chamber of Commerce, the Capital South Urban Redevelopment Corp. and the Columbus Area Growth Foundation. He has an undergraduate degree in history from Williams College and a master's degree in business administration from Stanford University's Graduate School of Business.

M. BRIAN McDONALD is director of the Bureau of Business and Economic Research at the University of New Mexico. The bureau is the major depository of economic and demographic data on New Mexico. Researchers at the bureau conduct programs specializing in short- and long-term state economic projections, western water resource issues and demographic projections for New Mexico. Before joining the bureau, McDonald was a research economist for Logistics Management Institute in Washington, D.C. McDonald received his undergraduate degree in economics from Georgetown University and his doctorate in economics from the University of Pennsylvania.

LEE R. McPHETERS, a professor of economics at Arizona State University since 1976, is the director of the University's Economic Outlook Center. The center specializes in economic forecasts for Arizona and the western United States. McPheters edits the *Arizona Blue Chip* and *Western Blue Chip* economic forecast newsletters, produced in collaboration with Bob Eggert. McPheters' numerous studies of the Arizona economy focus on issues such as tourism, transportation, criminal justice, high-tech manufacturing and the aviation industry. His current projects include a study of new business start-ups in the metropolitan Phoenix area. McPheters received his doctorate in economics from Virginia Polytechnic Institute.

GERALD P. O'DRISCOLL, JR., who chaired Session Four—The Southwest Economy: The Next Year and the Next Decade, is vice president and associate director of research at the Federal Reserve Bank of Dallas. He is an advisor on monetary policy to the president of the Dallas Fed and has general supervisory responsibility for the Dallas Fed's research department. He received his master's degree and doctorate in economics from the University of California at Los Angeles, and he taught economics at several universities. He has written numerous articles and papers on monetary economics, industrial organization and law and economics, plus several books. His most recent book, *Economics of Time and Ignorance*, written with co-author Mario J. Rizzo, received international attention.

HARVEY ROSENBLUM, who chaired Session Three—Critical Issues, is senior vice president and director of research for the Federal Reserve Bank of Dallas. He has been a key participant in the Dallas Fed's research on the international value of the dollar. He has also been instrumental in developing an index of leading economic indicators for Texas. In addition to two decades of service to the Federal Reserve System, Rosenblum has served several universities as a visiting professor. He now chairs the Advisory Council to the Department of Economics at Southern Methodist University. Rosenblum is the chief economic policy advisor to the Dallas Fed's president and is an associate economist for the Federal Open Market Committee.

PAUL F. ROTH is president of the Texas Division of Southwestern Bell Telephone Co. He has worked for Southwestern Bell since 1956, except for a brief period in 1977 when he served as director of public affairs for AT&T. After returning to Southwestern Bell, he served as president of the Arkansas Division, group president at Southwestern Bell Corp. and vice president of Finance and

External Affairs for Southwestern Bell Telephone. He is currently chairman of the State Advisory Council of Communities in School, a director of the Texas Research League and a board member of the Texas Chamber of Commerce and the Dallas Citizens Council. Roth holds a civil engineering degree from the University of Missouri; he attended graduate school at Washington University.

CONSUL GENERAL CARL E. RUFELDS is Canada's senior diplomat in the Southwest region of the United States. His area encompasses Texas, Louisiana, Arkansas, Oklahoma, New Mexico and Kansas. His posts during his 27-year career in foreign service for Canada include director of trade to Asia and the Pacific, senior trade commissioner and director of the U.S. Export Marketing Division. He has been stationed in Beirut, Milan, Bangkok, San Francisco, Guatemala, Peking and Ottawa. He received his degree in mechanical engineering from the University of Manitoba.

LOREN C. SCOTT is professor of economics and chairman of the Department of Economics at Louisiana State University. He received his bachelor's and master's degrees in economics from Texas Tech University and his doctorate in economics from Oklahoma State University. In addition to his teaching responsibilities, he has served Louisiana through his appointments to several state economic advisory boards, including the governor's Council on Economic Advisers. Scott is a prolific author and experienced lecturer. He was recently chosen as the Outstanding Teacher of M.B.A.'s by the Business Administration Leadership Council.

BARTON A. SMITH is chairman of the Department of Economics at the University of Houston. He also is an associate professor of economics and has been affiliated with the University of Houston since 1973. Smith served as director of the Center for Public Policy, and he continues to work with the center as a senior research associate. He received his bachelor's degree in political science from Brigham Young University and his master's degree and doctorate from the University of Chicago. Smith's research focuses on urban housing, transportation and environmental economics. During the past five years, his analyses of the Houston economy and real estate markets have received both national and local attention.

WILLIAM H. WALLACE is first vice president and chief operating officer of the Federal Reserve Bank of Dallas. With a doctorate in economics from the University of Illinois, he began his career in an academic capacity, serving as professor of economics for several universities. Wallace joined the Federal

Reserve System in 1967 at the Richmond Fed. He moved to the Board of Governors in Washington, D.C., in 1974, and he assumed his present position at the Dallas Fed in 1981. He serves in a variety of professional and civic organizations, including the American Economic Association, the American Statistical Association and the Dallas Committee on Foreign Relations. Wallace is chairman of the Education Committee of the Greater Dallas Chamber of Commerce and is president of the board of the Communities in Schools Program of Dallas.

KEREN WARE is director of the Office of Advanced Technology in the Business Development Division of the Texas Department of Commerce. Ware previously served as a research analyst and chief clerk of the Texas House of Representatives' Science and Technology Committee. In the spring of 1988, she took a leave of absence from the committee and traveled extensively through Asia and Australia to meet with more than 80 representatives of educational institutions, technology policy companies and high-tech businesses in six countries. She serves on the executive board of the Texas Alliance for Science, Technology and Mathematics Education and the board of the Texas Computer Industry Council. She is also a member of the Technology Industry Legislative Task Force and the Japan–American Society of Austin. Ware received her bachelor's degree in chemistry from Harvard University.

LARKIN WARNER is professor of economics at Oklahoma State University. He received his undergraduate training at Ohio Wesleyan University and was awarded a doctorate by Indiana University. He joined the OSU faculty in 1960 and served there until 1974, when he became director of the Economic Studies Division of the Kerr Foundation of Oklahoma City. Warner returned to OSU in 1979 to serve as the interim director of the Office of Business and Economic Research and director of the Center for Economic Education. His research focuses on Oklahoma's economic development and finance of state government. He recently was appointed to the Constitution Revision Study Commission, which will recommend changes to Oklahoma's state constitution.

The Southwest Economy in the 1990s:
A Different Decade

The 1990s:
A Different Decade

"Education is vital to future economic growth. For industries to prosper, they must have a highly educated labor force. Providing such a labor force will require some drastic changes in how we educate our young people."
—Robert H. Boykin

"One of the most important factors, if not the most important, to focus on is that we will be dealing with an integrated marketplace. We are no longer in the stage where a single area—cotton, cattle or energy—will fuel the economy."
—Admiral Bobby R. Inman

"Business leaders' interest is not limited to the professional schools or to science and engineering. They also want to hire graduates who have a broad, general education in the liberal arts."
—William H. Cunningham

"The tremendous reliance on energy, along with the breakneck pace of construction and almost uncontrolled lending by many thrifts in Texas, led to an overheated, overconcentrated growth environment, which had its inevitable consequences."
—John B. McCoy

Welcome Address—
The 1990s:
A Different Decade

Robert H. Boykin

During this conference, we will have an opportunity to look at some of the critical issues facing this part of the country and to hear ideas about how we might best deal with them. Our discussions will center on the Southwest region, which for our purposes includes Arizona, Louisiana, New Mexico, Oklahoma and Texas.

Each of these states has had its share of rude awakenings and economic gloom during the past few years. In many ways, we are a very different region economically in comparison with a few years ago. However, it would now appear that most of the region has entered a period of recovery—slow recovery, granted—but there seems to be a definite turn in the economic tide.

Those of you who were at our conference last year may recall that our chief economist, Harvey Rosenblum, stated that the Southwest is well situated for growth in the 1990s, but that many challenges remain. It is time to continue our assessment of the ways to reposition ourselves for a new and more prosperous era. That is why it is so important that we tackle these pressing challenges now— so we are better prepared to capitalize on the opportunities in our changing economic climate as we enter a new decade.

The topics we will discuss are those that are most crucial to the Southwest's economic well-being. You will note, for example, that a panel of experts is scheduled to consider the needs and challenges of education, which certainly has to be one of the top priorities not only here in the Southwest but also throughout the country. Education is vital to future economic growth. For industries to prosper, they must have a highly educated labor force. Providing such a labor force will require some drastic changes in how we educate our young people. Some important decisions will have to be made soon in this area.

Other important factors have a strong bearing on our economic growth in the Southwest, and at this conference we intend to face these issues head on. One of these issues concerns the role we will play in the international market-place. Economic performance in the Southwest will depend to a large extent on the growth of the economic base in each of the five states—that is, the sectors of each state's economy that provide goods and services to the rest of this country and to the rest of the world, such as manufacturing, services, agriculture, energy production and other resource extraction.

Growth in these sectors will increasingly depend on world market conditions; therefore, our Southwestern states must have the ability to compete on a worldwide basis. We must be prepared for these global challenges in the decade ahead to enable this area of the country to be competitive.

One part of our program will be a comprehensive session that will zero in on four crucial areas that will have a significant impact on economic growth here in the Southwest in the 1990s. Among the subjects our distinguished experts will discuss are

- *Financing Growth.* It is great to have all kinds of expansion plans for the future; that is good thinking, but do we know where the money will come from?
- *Technology.* We will learn what is new in technological innovation that will help us operate in the most efficient manner possible and, we hope, keep us ahead of the pack.
- *The Environment.* We have a vital need to maintain the quality of the environment, for environmental problems can most assuredly impose constraints on economic growth.
- *Energy.* Energy is another critical issue. It has a decisive impact on the economy in Louisiana, New Mexico, Oklahoma and Texas. So, learning how that industry is expected to perform in the next decade is important.

We are especially pleased to have such authoritative representatives from the five states comprising the great Southwest. These are the people who focus their attention on the economic pulse of their respective states. They will be sharing with us their projections on how their individual states will be faring in the next year and in the next decade.

Indeed, we are fortunate to have an impressive array of talent on the agenda of this conference. Each of our speakers is a recognized leader in his or her field and, therefore, will be able to give us meaningful views on issues to which we should be alert and on the action to take in preparation for the years ahead.

The very fact that you in the audience are committing your time to be here at this conference demonstrates your concern for the economic well-being of the Southwest and your interest in how we can improve this part of the world to make it a better place in which to live and work.

The Future of the Southwest Economy: Challenges and Opportunities

Admiral Bobby R. Inman

I spend a great deal of time traveling throughout this country. I had the privilege previously of spending about 22 years looking at the outside world. For almost seven years now, I have enjoyed the opportunity of intensively looking at my own country. The database is shallow, but the opinions are strongly held, and it is the latter that I am going to inflict on you at this conference.

First we should think about the 1990s. One of the most important factors, if not the most important, to focus on is that we will be dealing with an integrated marketplace. We are no longer in the stage where a single area—cotton, cattle or energy—will fuel the economy. All those elements will remain important. We have seen in this deep recession that we are just now edging out of very significant sustained growth in the service industries, particularly in tourism—industries that were vitally important in helping soften the impact of this long, deep recession. But I believe as we look into the 1990s, the certainty is that we must develop all segments of the economy, everything we can possibly push, if we are to have any reasonable prospect of even sustaining a standard of living for citizens in this region, much less any optimism that our children will enjoy, as we have, a steadily rising standard of living.

What causes me to reach that conclusion? Over the past six years, this great U.S. economy has created an aggregate of a little more than 8.8 million new jobs. That covers 1983 through 1987 into half of 1988. But as you look more closely at the numbers, you see that we created 10.4 million new jobs in what we loosely call the service sector. In the same time frame, we lost 1.2 million jobs in manufacturing and 400,000 jobs in mining. The average weekly wage of the 10.4 million new jobs in the service sector was $272. The average weekly wage in the 1.6 million jobs lost was $444. Even accepting that U.S. workers may have

5

been overpaid in relation to their peers abroad, the reality is that for a significant number of our citizens who are working, the standard of living has already begun to decline. So, we cannot count on simply expanding service industries as the way to sustain a standard of living.

As you look at the fact that in developing an integrated marketplace, it is an *international* marketplace; changes in the outside world dramatically affect the possibilities. Unhappily, much as we might like to think we can, we do not control many of the developments in the outside world. We have to be prepared to accommodate them, to alter our own strategy as they occur. And they are not little changes. When the title was chosen for this conference, "The 1990s: A Different Decade," I am not sure even the authors realized how different the 1990s are going to be in the outside world.

Daily we are watching changes in the Soviet Union, in Eastern Europe, even in China, that were not forecasted, even as recently as 1988 in many cases. Nor do we have any certainty where those changes will go. China certainly has reminded us of that fact.

Beginning in the late 1970s, we watched the Chinese embark on an effort to shift the nature of their economy—to pay much more attention to what we would consider consumer goods. They began in agriculture with great success—moving from a country that had a long history of repeated famines and starvation to one that even now has the ability to export food. They moved to the cities. They tried to let the marketplace begin to respond to the stimulation of free enterprise, but perhaps they moved too swiftly—first with three, then with 14 cities—while holding a doctrinaire, communist approach to government. The result was that they did not have the talent in place to manage the change. They began to have all the difficulties that occur when change is not properly managed—corruption, disaffection. They also were trying to introduce the technologies that are so important in the face of change, like fax machines. They found that facilitating economic change also raises the specter of political change. The old generation that still governs China simply could not cope with the political change, and thus came the crackdown on June 3 in Tiananmen Square.

I dwell on China because we are watching the most remarkable series of events in the Soviet Union and in Eastern Europe—shared political power for the first time in 40-plus years in Poland. And there may also be a more pertinent factor: sharing the blame for economic failure as well as for political opportunity. We have in Hungary the renaming of the republic, renaming of the party, even some indication of permitting multiple parties—something thus far not tolerated for any extended period in any country ruled by the Communist Party. One-party control has been the single most critical element of maintaining its posture.

It is far too early to make any reasoned judgment on where these changes will take us. Will they take us to a point where there are new market opportunities and some kind of convertibility of the ruble that makes it prudent for U.S. businesses to begin to look at expanding? Or will it simply be a place where we pour a lot more public aid, increase the debt and see little change? Or will, in fact, we see the opening that is now so encouraging politically be replaced by the same leaders with great repression if they believe they are approaching the edge of chaos?

Now, the good news. Throughout the world, we find people prepared to declare that the cold war is dead and that we are in a very different era. Well, we *are* in a different era: one where even if those changes had not been occurring in the Soviet Union, in Eastern Europe and in China, our attention would increasingly be drawn to some very troublesome prospective changes in much of the rest of the world in the nature of potential hostilities.

For a very long time we have been in a relatively stable global environment. Five powers had nuclear weapons, and they all understood clearly the controls that should be maintained, and they had a great reluctance to use those weapons. Did any of you see on television this morning the story on Israeli–South African collaboration on nuclear weapons and ballistic missiles? I did not stage that or plant that story to coincide with this conference. But it underlines a principal point: the 1980s have produced a proliferation of ballistic missiles around the world. China is selling them to Saudi Arabia; Israel is developing them; Argentina is developing them; and South Africa, with or without Israeli collaboration, has been producing ballistic missiles. The Soviets and others have sold missiles. Iraq took short-range missiles and significantly expanded their capacity. Along with that, count the proliferation of nuclear warheads. There are probably five, six, maybe even seven additional countries that either have nuclear weapons already or have the capacity to produce them. With that has come an enormous proliferation in the capacity to produce chemical weapons. In the Middle East in the Iran–Iraq war, we saw it move beyond just proliferation to use.

The reality going into the 1990s is that in much of the world, there is now a potential for using weapons of mass destruction in a regional conflict in ways that did not exist in the past. There is no great certainty going into the decade that a more reasoned approach will prevail in areas where ancient tribal or religious feuds and hatreds have fueled recurring conflicts over the past 40 years while we have avoided global conflict.

We have the reality of a huge debt in many of the less-developed countries—largely public debt held with private banks in the United States, in

Western Europe, and to a significantly lesser degree, in Japan. Many of the economies with which we might otherwise hope to interact in the international marketplace in the 1990s simply will not be able to be participants until something is done to alter very significantly their ability to invest.

Terrorism has not run its course. Unhappily, those who participate in international terrorist activities increasingly are aligned with those who manufacture and distribute drugs. The whole issue of international production and transfer of drugs is a growing problem. Our part in that is that we remain the world's largest consumer of drugs, just as we are the world's largest consumer market in many areas. But we have some major problems to solve. Even if all those activities were not occurring to raise challenges for the 1990s, we have very dramatic changes coming on the economic landscape.

In 1992, Europe is slated to take down internal barriers to the flow of goods, services and workers. Over a period of years, it would become the world's largest market and, thus, replace the United States, which has occupied that role for a very long time. In East Asia, we are continuing to see a tremendous spurt of economic growth. But we are also beginning to see a shift of political leadership. A generation that has governed the nations of Asia, which have shown such tremendous economic growth over the past 20 years to 25 years, is now beginning to leave. In Japan, an accelerated political transition has been caused by a series of scandals, the largest the Japanese have encountered in the postwar era. We still do not know a lot about the leadership evolving in that country, one of our closest allies. But there are at least some early signs that this new generation of political leadership will be more nationalistic, perhaps more arrogant about Japan's economic power and less concerned about accommodating the interests of its principal military ally.

Given that uncertain and rapidly changing world where we clearly want to anchor significant growth in the 1990s, what should we do? Clearly, we need access to markets. That is going to make our relationships with Europe very important as they evolve in the 1990s. It is going to mean working out our relationships in East Asia in ways that encourage continued access to markets— to open markets that are now closed. It is going to make it very important that we keep some focus on solving the Third World debt problem to ensure the genuine potential for growth of markets in Latin America, in Africa and indeed in Eastern Europe.

Let me suggest one item, though close to home, that I believe should be very high on our agenda in the 1990s. I am a strong believer, from having raised a couple of teen-agers, that incentives work better over the long term than punishment. I am persuaded that this is true in dealing with nations as well. There are times when you have to turn to punishment, but incentives are better.

At the beginning of 1989, we implemented a historic agreement that was, in fact, the subject of an election in Canada in November 1988. It is the U.S.–Canada Free Trade Agreement, which will take a good while to phase in. I believe a sustained, carefully structured move toward bringing Mexico into that trade agreement should be near the top of our agenda for dealing with the outside world. It will not be easy. Mexico has a very different economy, and it will be significantly harder to integrate. But such a North American market clearly would again be the largest market in the world, with all the attractions it would bring for other countries to want to work constructively, as opposed to getting into an environment of barriers.

Those are things we need to do in dealing with the outside world. What do we need to do here at home to be ready to deal with the challenges and the opportunities of the 1990s? The question applies to the country at large. It applies particularly to the Southwest region.

We need reliable sources of capital at affordable rates. We cannot be competitive in the international marketplace if our cost of capital continues to be very significantly higher than that of the countries with which we will compete. This high cost of capital particularly affects issues of modernization and expansion of our manufacturing capacity.

We must have a skilled *and* motivated work force. Education is the front line. I am particularly delighted that the first panel of this conference will confront the education issues directly, and I will have a little more to say about our status before I close. *Skilled* only deals with part of what is needed; the other part is *motivation.* There are a lot of things that go into that, including the issue of access to and use of drugs and the demotivation they have on a work force.

We must have a strong base of science and be at the cutting edge of converting that science into usable technology. That makes the combination of investment by the federal government and the private sector critically important. We must have policies that ensure sustained investment, but we also must focus to ensure that we have access to ongoing, state-of-the-art research activity in this region if we hope to be at the forefront of economic growth in the 1990s.

There are some additional factors that will be critically important to economic growth in the 1990s. Quality—the focus on quality must be unremitting. My evidence is anecdotal, but I at least am persuaded by it. We have had three and one-half years now of sustained effort to talk down the value of the dollar and hold it at a lower level to help our ability to export. For many of our industries, the strategy has been very, very successful. The U.S. trade deficit, however, remains very, very large. The large volume of imports to the United States is not made up of cheap goods coming from underdeveloped countries. These imports are products from the countries most affected by the change in the value of the dollar.

U.S. consumers have voted with their pocketbooks. Until the U.S. consumer judges U.S. products to be of comparable or better quality than imports, how can we honestly demand from other countries that they pressure their citizens to buy products where those who voted by spending made a judgment that the quality will not match? So, we have to make a sustained effort across the board for both the perception and the reality of U.S. goods and services to be that they are at least as good in quality as any others produced in the world on a sustained basis—zero defect has to be the goal. Companies with real dedication to quality always have experienced trepidation about whether they could afford the cost. What they have discovered is that a commitment to quality is cost-effective as well as enormously effective in the market.

An issue that has received much less attention than quality, but is parallel to it, is safety. As I look at the reality of growing concerns about the workplace, about health-care costs that continue to burgeon, and about the environment, I think that a sustained focus on safety—of individuals, of the environment, of the workplace—will be a very critical factor in economic success and growth in the 1990s.

I began with some remarks on the standard of living. We have enjoyed a higher standard of living than most other countries, and that was made possible, in part, because productivity was higher in the United States. But productivity has not kept pace with the changes. Unless we are successful broadly in improving the productivity of the work force, many of our other efforts ultimately will not be successful.

I mentioned earlier the science and technology base. If we are to have an opportunity to develop that to our advantage, we have to focus on protecting intellectual property much more successfully than we have in the past. That leads me to the final issue on this list of things we must do inside this region. We have to come to grips with what a litigious society we have become. With great apologies to those in the legal profession who are with us, one statistic always gets my attention as I compare the economic performance of the United States and Japan. We have 10 lawyers for each one the Japanese have, and they have five engineers on the factory floor for each one we have. I am not advocating that we do everything in parallel, but I suggest to you that we are way out of balance on both sides of the equation. Also, the associated costs are ultimately a very significant factor in our ability to compete effectively in an international marketplace.

What must we do here in this region—early? We need to attack a good many of these issues. I will not get into my own views on the specifics of education because the learned panel is going to do that shortly, but let me suggest at least as a broad goal that we need to look now at putting in place critical infrastructure improvements for sustaining economic growth.

I have been troubled, in my now almost seven years living in this region after 33 years' absence, to find significant pockets of the population that really are comfortable with what they have and very reluctant to support investment to ensure growth. They do not want to deal with change. They are *very* comfortable with what they have. But we cannot stand still. Stagnation develops and then comes a decline. If we are not able to develop and sustain momentum for economic growth, we will see a long period of decline. Some of the investment and infrastructure has to come from the state and from localities. Some will come from the federal government, although I suspect that through the 1990s the overall percentage of real-dollar investment coming to this area from the federal government will continue to decline. We will have to focus much more on what we do here in the region in dealing with these issues.

Particularly for us in the Southwest, we have the challenge of the realities of demographic change. The birthrate for young Anglo women of childbearing age is holding at about 1.7; the birthrate for young black women of childbearing age was 2.3 earlier in the decade and is now tracking at about 2.5, where it appears to be stable; and the birthrate for young Hispanic women, which was 2.7 earlier in the decade and is now at 2.9, may even pass 3. In a significant portion of that Hispanic growth, two or sometimes even three of those youngsters are born before the mother is 20 years old. That tells us that we have some very major challenges in both health and education in dealing with the reality of a work force that is going to change dramatically. Just from those demographic changes, setting aside immigration, we will have somewhere in this region in the mid-1990s—maybe not in Oklahoma, but probably in Louisiana and certainly in the rest of the region—the likelihood that if we are able to keep the youngsters in school to the 12th grade level, more than half those entering the work force and eligible to enter the work force, will be non-Anglo. Looking at the base needed to draw from in mathematics, science and engineering to sustain the growth of that science and technology base, we will have to develop a very significantly enhanced portion of that pool of talent from those who are on the lower side of the economic base at the present time.

So, we are not just confronting a problem and developing ways to overcome it; we have to come to grips with demographic change. I dwell on this issue because of an experience three years ago here in Dallas when I talked to a group of school superintendents from Texas. That was after all those years of being away. I was struck by a response from a school superintendent from a district near Wichita Falls. He protested my criticism of the overall performance of the education system in Texas. His specific assertion was that, in fact, the scores and the performance of Texas students are as good as any in the country: it is when you include all the minorities and immigrants that the picture changes. If you get that kind of attitude from a school superintendent, even one in a mixed rural and suburban area in the 1980s, just think about the 1990s and the need to come to grips with the composition of a skilled and motivated work force.

Finally, we must have coherent public policy that focuses on the need to build and sustain economic growth throughout the period. That is never easy to accomplish unless there is great need. As a nation, we have a great record for responding in time of crisis with coherent public policy that focuses on solving the problems. When we do not have a sense of urgency, it is much harder. In this region, we still lack a sense of urgency about the need to invest in infrastructure, the need to significantly raise the level of education, or the need to create the infrastructure that will sustain economic growth. We see in California some interesting new approaches to public policy to ensure private investment for the long term. It is not yet clear to me that we will be prepared to deal coherently with those issues here. We cannot tell you the answers from the Federal Reserve System. The Federal Reserve System exists to support and help sustain a strong financial system, to focus on critical issues not only in stabilizing that system but also in dealing with inflation. But we hope that those of you who have gathered here will, on your own, begin to realize how you affect the development of public policies in this region to ensure that we will come to grips now with the problems of the 1990s before, rather than after, the crises overwhelm us.

Research and Public Service in Comprehensive Universities

William H. Cunningham

I would like to speak to you about the changing role in society of major, comprehensive research universities. The term *comprehensive* describes an institution that has bachelor's, master's and doctoral programs. Research implies that the institution's mission extends beyond classroom education and that it makes a significant contribution to the nation's fundamental research effort. While I am sure it will come as no surprise to you, I will use the University of Texas at Austin as my example and as a case study.

The University of Texas at Austin is committed to the pursuit of high standards of achievement in instruction, student performance, research and scholarly accomplishment. Our mission is to promote the development of the human resources of Texas and of the nation to their highest potential. That development is translated into the three fundamental components of the University's mission: teaching, research and public service. While undergraduate and graduate education have always been of paramount importance to the mission of the institution, I would like to speak to you today about the growing and evolving responsibilities the University must address in basic research and public service.

A large percentage of the basic research conducted in the United States is carried out in our great universities. That is, quite simply, a matter of national policy. Major universities, with the support of the federal government and the private sector, focus their efforts on basic research, while the corporate and industrial communities focus resources on applied research.

Today, 100 universities conduct approximately 60 percent of the nation's basic research. I suggest that, if you examine the data more closely, you will discover that most basic research at the university level is done by no more than 20 institutions. In 1989, the University of Texas at Austin will spend more than

$150 million on basic research, and it clearly is one of those 20 institutions.

Basic research is important because it is a critical element of graduate instruction. One-on-one interaction between faculty and student in the classroom, in the laboratory and in the development of a master's or doctoral thesis lies at the heart of the graduate experience.

Our nation's drive to remain competitive in world markets also centers on basic research. Basic research is the feedstock of applied research, research that is conducted in the laboratories of corporate America. Without basic research, new products produced by Americans, working in American companies, would not be competitive with those produced abroad. I strongly believe that basic research is far too important to be left to any one sector of the nation. However, until American companies are wise enough to look beyond the immediacy of next quarter's profits and invest in basic research, universities will have no choice but to conduct a disproportionate amount of this country's basic research.

As the research role of the institution has expanded, it has become ever more interrelated with its public-service component, a phenomenon summarized under the buzzword *economic development*. The University for many years has had a major involvement in four areas of economic development. The first area, and still the most important, is education. The University educates a large number of excellent undergraduate and graduate students each year. That will always be the University's strongest contribution to economic development.

The second way the University traditionally contributes to economic development is through the work of research centers such as the Bureau of Economic Geology, the Bureau of Business Research and the Bureau of Engineering Research.

The third way the University contributes to the economic health of our state is through the transfer of technology from University laboratories to the marketplace. Traditionally, the University accomplished this through patents and license agreements. In addition, during the past two years, three new corporations have been established to commercialize products that are the result of technology created in University laboratories. We are negotiating the establishment of a fourth new corporation. In each case, the professor who created the invention owns part of the firm, the University owns a share and a venture capitalist who is willing to invest his or her own money to support further research in the project owns a share.

The fourth way the University stimulates economic development is through its assistance in attracting new businesses to Texas. Corporate leaders want to locate businesses in communities with first-rate educational programs. They want their employees and their families to have ready access to such institutions.

In addition, they need to interact with faculty consultants and recruit highly educated undergraduate and graduate students.

Business leaders' interest is not limited to the professional schools or to science and engineering. They also want to hire graduates who have a broad, general education in the liberal arts. In addition, corporate leaders want to locate in communities with rich and varied cultural opportunities. Quality of life is not a frill; it is a necessity. Citizens want to attend lyric operas, Broadway productions, ballets and art exhibitions; they want to participate in symposia on the timely and timeless issues of the day.

While it is apparent to many that the University has been involved in economic development for many years, in 1983 Admiral Bob Inman and Microelectronics and Computer Technology Corp. (MCC) came to Austin, and the University has never been the same. No longer a passive participant, the University became an active player in the state's attempt to recruit MCC. The University agreed to permit MCC's proposed building to be constructed on land at the University's Balcones Research Center, and the University guaranteed the construction financing that was to come from private-sector donations.

Another recent example of the University's contribution to economic development is the recruitment of Sematech. When the opportunity came to become a partner in attracting a major public-private semiconductor research consortium to Austin, the University was no longer merely an active player; it became a lead player. The University had an outstanding and expanding program in materials science and microelectronics. In addition, the University offered to purchase a research facility, renovate it and guarantee the bonds for the project.

A third example of the University's role in economic development is the superconducting super collider (SSC). Dr. Peter Flawn, our president emeritus, chaired the Texas National Research Laboratory Commission that drafted the state proposal to the federal government. Dr. Herbert Woodson, dean of engineering, was the vice chairman of the commission. Most of the work was completed at the University's Bureau of Economic Geology. In addition, when the commission lacked sufficient funds to begin the project, the University loaned it $70,000 so it could begin its work in a timely manner.

Other people, including Governor Bill Clements; Mort Meyerson, who became chairman of the commission when Dr. Flawn resigned; and Tom Luce, who became chairman when Mr. Meyerson stepped down, clearly played a role in the recruitment of the SSC. Still, I believe it is accurate to state that the University played a key role, if not the key role, in attracting the SSC to Texas.

I have focused on the changing role of a major comprehensive research university in society. I have tried to point out that, while teaching is and always has been central to the mission of the institution, the University also plays a major role in basic research and economic development.

I would like to conclude by citing a classic example of the interaction between teaching, research and economic development. The Center for Electromechanics, located at the University's Balcones Research Center, is directed by Professor Bill Weldon. The center has been largely responsible for the development and creation of new ways to store massive amounts of energy and then to release this energy in an intense electrical pulse in a fraction of a second. This research was initiated to provide a pulse-power source for high-field magnets needed for the University's fusion research program.

Although this application was never implemented, the University's laboratories developed an electrical machine, called a *homopolar generator*, and it led to the development of the railgun. The *railgun* is just what its name implies. It is a gun that fires a projectile down two copper rails and uses an arc of electricity to move the projectile at hypervelocity speeds, approximately 21,000 feet per second. To place this number in perspective, a high-velocity rifle fires a bullet at about 3,000 feet per second.

With the development of railgun technology, research has come full circle. Scientists now believe that the railgun can be used to generate fusion energy in the laboratory. That is, if the scientist could propel a projectile fast enough against a solid object, it is theoretically possible to generate thermonuclear fusion energy upon impact. Researchers are investigating this hypothesis today at the University.

The railgun research has also developed several new applications. For example, the gun has substantial military uses associated with the Strategic Defense Initiative (SDI) and advanced weaponry systems. The homopolar generator that powers the railgun is able to produce, for a fraction of a second, approximately 80 percent of the power of South Texas Nuclear One. It sits on a platform that is smaller than 10 feet in diameter. Using the homopolar generator to drive the railgun permits a steel projectile to penetrate approximately 16 inches of hardened steel. Another example of its power is that if a hypervelocity railgun were fired upward, the projectile would not come back; it would go into orbit.

When General James A. Abrahamson, who was at the time in charge of all SDI projects for the federal government, was in Austin to inspect the railgun, he asked Professor Weldon, in my presence, how long it took to recharge the homopolar generator. In essence, the question was, "What happens if we miss and have to reload?" Professor Weldon told him it took about one and one-half minutes to bring the homopolar generator up to full power after it has been fired.

General Abrahamson said this could represent a problem in a military crisis.

At that point, Professor Weldon indicated that he would like to show the general the University's newest invention, the *compulsator*. The compulsator is half the size of a homopolar generator and produces twice the power of South Texas Nuclear One, and it can be fired 60 times a second. General Abrahamson was duly impressed.

The work that is being done at the University's Center for Electromechanics provides several important lessons. First, we never know where basic research will lead us. In this case, Professor Weldon's research has gone from fusion, to SDI, to commercial research and back to fusion.

Professor Weldon now has a major contract with the Department of Defense to develop a new pulse-power generator that will produce 1 percent of the installed generating capacity of the world in a field-portable machine to be located on a vehicle. To repeat, the new field-portable, pulse-power generator will produce 1 percent of the installed generating capacity of the world.

Second, basic research leads to commercial applications. For example, using pulse power enabled us to create new metal alloys that could not be produced before. In addition, metal powders can be formed into solid metal parts, and thin films of metal can be sprayed onto surfaces. One particularly interesting application involves using this power source for welding. Two large metal sections can be welded together in less than a tenth of a second, and the strength of the resulting weld is identical to the original metal. The applications range from major pipe-welding projects, such as the Alaska pipeline, to regular drill pipe.

Third, University basic research can help strengthen the Texas economy and attract much-needed federal dollars. The Center for Electromechanics receives approximately $10 million per year from the federal government. It has already spent more than $55 million of contract funds, and it has about $11 million of contracts under way.

Fourth, basic research can help diversify the state's economy. The homopolar generator is being commercially manufactured in Midland, Texas, by Parker Kinetics, and it has been sold to major companies such as General Dynamics. The University receives a royalty payment with each sale of a homopolar generator.

Fifth, basic research is central to providing many of our best students with excellent educational opportunities. Twenty-six undergraduates and 10 graduate students work at the Center for Electromechanics. In addition, Professor Weldon is supervising seven doctoral students.

Sixth, basic research can play an important role in this nation's defense. The University is developing an all-electric tank that would fire weapons using small compulsators.

   I hope that I have been able to provide you with a sense of the role that your university, the University of Texas at Austin, plays in the nation's basic research effort as well as in the state's drive to diversify its economy. Undergraduate and graduate education will never lose their rightful position of importance at the University, yet the University, like most other dynamic public enterprises, must adjust to the ever-changing requirements that society places on it.

From Outlook to Opportunity: Making the 1990s Work

John B. McCoy

I think we all must have a bit of honesty when we talk about what is going on with the economy. And I must say that after six months in Texas, we feel very good about our opportunities. After the talks and discussions of the past two days here, I suspect that most, if not all, of you have as many thoughts about the economy as I do. At the risk of preaching to the converted, I would like to say that Banc One is betting on the Texas economy. We are here because we believe its best days lie ahead.

By year-end, we will have completed acquisition of MCorp, whose 20 banks across the state we have been running under a management contract with the Federal Deposit Insurance Corp. since last July. This franchise makes up one of the largest commercial banking organizations in Texas. It also represents our largest acquisition ever.

Tom Hoaglin is the current chief executive officer of Bank One, Texas. Tom ran Bank One, Dayton, the top financial performer among all our banks in 1988, at a return on assets in excess of 1.7 percent. When he took over the bank, it had a return on assets of 1.4 percent, and I thought if he would just maintain that, that would be good. So, we have great expectations for Tom.

But aside from Tom and a team of our best financial people, Bank One, Texas, is going to be run by Texans already here. Keeping the best Texas people has not always been easy. As soon as we received our notice that we had won the bid for MCorp in June, we came down to meet the folks. We were met very cheerfully at the airport by one of the local bank executives, Jim Gardner. As we started driving to town, he said, "I want to be straightforward with you; I'm leaving the company." When I asked him why, he said that among the six banks that bid for MCorp, four had offered him a job, and we were not one of the four.

Well, I realized that if he quit then and there, we would not be able to find our way through the town, let alone run the banks. So, I explained to Jim (who is here and is our vice chairman), "Jim, you know we are not very smart, and I want you to understand we never thought of offering you a job. And I want you to understand we didn't think of not offering you a job." We spent the day together, and I am happy to say that Jim said, "I think I like that style." Needless to say, Jim is with us today and is our head Texan, so to speak.

We are looking forward to joining and contributing to renewed growth in the Texas economy. The signs I am reading are all pointing in the right direction.

I think one of the things that intensified the impact of the economic downturn here was that Texas had come so far, so fast. Take just one example: the unemployment rate. For about 10 years through 1985, the Texas unemployment rate was consistently below that for the country as a whole, sometimes by more than 2 full percentage points. The tremendous reliance on energy, along with the breakneck pace of construction and almost uncontrolled lending by many thrifts in Texas, led to an overheated, overconcentrated growth environment, which had its inevitable consequences. But if surface indicators made conditions seem better during the boom than they actually were when oil and gas went into sharp decline and unemployment grew to as much as 40 percent higher than the national rate in 1986 and 1987, the prospects for recovery seemed weaker than they actually were. I use the word *seemed* advisedly because now, in my view, we are at the threshold of a turnaround.

I see a region here that has come through some very difficult times, a victim of some rough economic change. Few people outside Texas know how devastating the economic fall has been for Texans on a personal level. Everybody knows someone who has had to take personal bankruptcy. This individual hardship cuts to a depth reminiscent to many people of the 1930s, when businessmen lost everything and had to rebuild their lives from scratch. I tried to explain to our board of directors this devastation that I have seen in Texas; I do not believe that it is comprehended in the Midwest and other places. The way I tried to describe it to our board—and I think it shocked them—is; "Imagine we were in Texas in 1980 and the 15 of you who are the outstanding citizens of the Midwest had gone through this. In eight years, 1988, three of you would have taken bankruptcy. I believe three more of you will have to take bankruptcy. Six of you probably lost half of your net worth." And this shocked them.

But probably the biggest surprise that I have seen in Texas is this devastation on a personal level. And we have to work, all of us have to work, to build up that spirit. I mean it really is to me very much like the Depression. One of our finest directors, who died at the age of 90 after winning two World Series and two Kentucky Derbys, took bankruptcy in the Depression and was able to come back. I think that there will be a lot of good people who have taken bankruptcy that we have to help come back to build this economy.

Revival of the economy and renewal of Texas financial institutions will not occur overnight. Loan demand may be sluggish. We estimate loan growth of 5 percent per year for the time being as many businesses and consumers try to continue to live within their cash flow and avoid incremental debt. Recuperation of the state's real estate industry may be long term, but the overall direction of the Texas economy is up. I believe the real challenge in reaping the benefits of that long-term growth is to maintain realism and economic flexibility.

While continued change is the one constant in commercial life, we have to make change work for us. At Banc One, we equate Texas with unprecedented opportunity. For some 20 years, we have grown by acquiring good small- to medium-size Midwestern banks, even a few large Midwestern banks. That formula led us from one bank in Columbus, Ohio, to 52 affiliates in Ohio, Indiana, Kentucky, Wisconsin and Michigan. We bring out the best in their people by setting strong financial and customer service standards and letting the people do the job.

In Texas, we have entered the third-largest state economy and the fifth-largest banking market in the United States. Dallas, Fort Worth and Houston comprise the eighth-largest banking market in the country. In the aggregate, they are almost as large a banking market as our entire Ohio market. Dallas and Houston alone make up the 10th-largest banking market nationwide. You must believe we are not going to take the eye off the ball down here. Our host, the Federal Reserve Bank of Dallas, has kept as sensitive a finger on the pulse of the Southwest economy as anyone I know. The talks and discussions here of the last day and a half have drawn a detailed picture of the Southwest economy and the outlook for Texas.

But I would like to emphasize three factors to which I give special importance because they are closely related to how banks will have a significant role in nourishing the Texas economy. One is the growing diversity of business and industry here. The Dallas–Fort Worth metropolitan complex, as you know, already reflects a more diverse economy than other commercial centers in Texas. It has already recovered most of the ground lost in the mid-1980s. A healthy banking system geared to provide capital to starting and expanding small businesses will be an important catalyst for enhancing future growth, increasing diversity on a statewide basis and, in the process, further reducing dependence on the oil and gas industry. It will also help to lower the vacancy rate in those handsome office buildings.

The second factor is expected population growth. Texas is the third-largest center of population in the United States. Over the past 30 years or so, the Texas population has nearly doubled, a rate of increase twice that of the United States as a whole. In 1987 and 1988, the rest of the country's population grew at a greater rate than this state's did, but not much greater. In looking at the estimates through the year 2000, Ohio is expected to have zero growth; growth in Wisconsin is supposed to be down 1 percent, and Indiana is supposed to have 1-percent growth. So again, I think that you can see the opportunity that Texas represents to us. Now, the rebuilding economy promises to move the Texas growth rate out ahead of the rest of the country again. This will have a positive effect on the housing industry—an area, I need not tell you, in which a healthy banking system plays a key role.

Third, Texas is joining the shift in the nation's business and industrial profile away from manufacturing and heavy industry to an economy based on services. To me, this signals great opportunity for the addition and application of new technologies—and from my own practical, parochial point of view—especially those related to responsible financial management, both commercial and personal.

The restructured MCorp franchise we are in the process of acquiring is represented in all major Texas markets, as well as more diverse and diversifying markets statewide. The franchise is the second largest in the Dallas–Fort Worth metropolitan market. A strong, loyal customer base of many consumers and businesses has remained with us. Our asset structure, marked to current market from $13 billion to approximately $10 billion, is lean and mean. Nonperforming assets are nonexistent. Our own financial systems, in effect in our five other states, have been installed throughout the Bank One, Texas, network. We are ready to go.

For all that, we would not be here—I would not be talking to you today—but for one thing: the quality of the people in the organization we are acquiring. If that sounds too oversimplified, a little overdramatic, let me explain by taking you back a bit. Two things have worked for us over the years. First, we acquire banks run by managers with proven track records. Set the money and the paper aside; a bank is people. We centralize the paper-related operations, provide a supportive culture of sharing of ideas among our banks and set very specific and closely monitored financial performance targets. The local management, who knows its market, is in charge of the bank. All the acquisitions we have made over 20 years were made because of the quality of management in place. And the opposite is true. Of the acquisitions we did not make, 80 percent involved a lack of confidence in management.

The second thing that has worked for us is that we stick to what we do best— retail and middle-market lending—and the place we know best—the Midwest. We think like small-town bankers, lending only in our markets and generally not trying to do things we do not know how to do. That has kept us from many exotic opportunities offered by our big city banking acquaintances and left us free of many mistakes. It is one of the reasons that we are probably the largest bank in the country with no foreign loans; we never could figure out how to loan in South America.

About two years ago, several of our senior people told me we really should take a look at Texas. It did not sound like that great an idea to me at the time. Texas was well out of our region and not a banking environment driven by retail and middle-market banking. But the way we operate our company (kind of management by dissent, if you will) inspired them to persist. I was still reluctant. But I also knew that just looking could not cost us much. So we did look. We actually talked to MCorp people, and they asked us whether we would put up $200 million infusion of capital. That did not appeal to us. Then time passed, and the opportunity arose to place a bid with the FDIC to acquire the assets of the Bridge Bank representing MCorp. At that time, I still did not see how we could integrate the MCorp banks into our structure and system. But I told our people to go ahead and look; looking does not cost very much.

During our due diligence, a team of 12 analysts and executives studied the operations of MCorp. We were struck from the beginning by the quality of the people we found. Our accounting guy said, "The controls aren't good, but I'm impressed by the people," and the next guy said something similar. So, we went back to focus on the people, how they got there, who the boss was, why they had not left. We were struck by the fact that the best people had remained and had somehow retained their motivation. It appeared to us that they knew that they would emerge as survivors. Our team wound up interviewing the top people at every bank. At some of the banks they went 40 people to 60 people deep, and we found out just how good the people at those banks are. That is when I really got interested in Texas.

It is just not our style to go in and replace management. This philosophy dates back many years ago to when my father was running the bank. One day the head of the largest bank in Cleveland called and said, "John, would you be interested if we could take my bank and your bank and the bank in Cincinnati and put them together? We will have the strongest organization in Ohio. What a great opportunity." My father said, "That would be the niftiest thing we could do." And they arranged to have breakfast for secrecy. My father said, "Why don't you come out to the house? My wife will fix you breakfast and we can talk about this." So, the guy came down. They were having breakfast and my father said, "Now, do I understand this correctly? You suggest that we will put your bank and my bank and the bank in Cincinnati together?" And the guy said, "That's absolutely what we want to do." And my father said, "What would you like me to do in the new company?" The guy said, "We won't need you." Well, that was one of the shortest breakfasts my father held. And he started right then and there in finding out how you involve people in making sure there is a place for those people. That is really how our philosophy on acquisitions got started and why we want current management to run the banks, not somebody else.

There are many examples of how this people-first strategy works. With the same people, our Banc One affiliate in Indianapolis went from 0.95 percent to 1.55 percent return on assets in three years after the acquisition. In Wisconsin, the acquired banks under the same management went from 0.96 percent to 1.35 percent return on assets in 18 months. Our overall return on average assets systemwide is 1.43 percent. That is among the best in the banking business and is achieved by local management running its own banks. I just cannot reiterate that enough. We acquired American Fletcher three years ago, a bank that never earned more than 1 percent return on assets. Last year, it earned 1.55 percent return on assets. Every member of its senior staff who was with the bank the day we acquired the bank, which was basically everyone, is still there today. So, they did it themselves. We actually sent one person from Columbus to that bank. And if you think one guy can outwit 3,000, you are wrong. He put in our financial system. Do you know where that one person is today? He is down here, and he is our chief financial officer. We have put in our financial system so that we can have the local people run the bank.

The decision to go to Texas was easy. The hard part was leaving our Midwest-only strategy and convincing ourselves to go to a state known for large corporate banking, commercial real estate and energy lending. We had to be convinced that Texas had markets for retail and middle-market lending.

We are retail and middle-market bankers, doing small business loans, student loans, home mortgages, automobile loans, trust services, consumer finance, equipment leasing, discount brokerage, data processing and so forth. Our net interest margin of 5.3 so far in 1989 is among the best in banking. We operate our branches more like stores than traditional banks; we concentrate on product sales to meet income targets. We are like McDonald's. Our stores have a lot in common, a lot of compatibility. We are not selling chicken in one place and steaks in another. We are selling the same thing everywhere. And like McDonald's, we stick to what we do best. We are not about to open a French restaurant in Texas.

But our analysis of the Texas banking market convinced us that here *is* a retail and middle-market banking environment brimming with opportunity—a market in the midst of dynamic change that will reshape its fundamental character. And new competitors, both in state and out of state, perceive the same opportunity.

This is how we see it in Texas. First, we believe the domination of retail market distribution by thrifts will shift to commercial banks. Despite its big population in major metropolitan complexes, Texas is a banking market in which the traditional means of competition for consumer accounts have been limited by law for commercial banks. The result is that thrifts have dominated distribution of consumer services and, because of the crucial importance of the convenience factor, dominated the consumer market. Thrifts have also fragmented the consumer market to a degree unknown in branch-banking states. Commercial banks will purchase and consolidate major market share in Texas by both buying thrifts and expanding retail operations in the faster-growing areas.

Second, Texas lending stands to benefit greatly from the introduction of home-equity financing, prevalent in other states. Proposed legislation in Texas will allow home-equity financing products widely available elsewhere. We believe that the availability to individuals of credit secured by the equity in their homes will stimulate badly needed loan growth in Texas, as it has nationally. The addition of this product will also offer individuals the tax advantage of home-equity financing. We see this as a major opportunity, particularly in the executive and professional retail market, which in Texas continues to rely on personal balance sheet and cash flow analysis.

Third, the Texas credit market will expand as revitalized banks reclaim their former card customers. One of the first things Bank One, Texas, will do is to rebuild the portfolio of direct credit card customers of the former MCorp organization. Like other Texas commercial banks, MCorp sold its own credit card portfolio to Lomas and Nettleton. Bank One recently mailed 123,000 short-form credit card applications to current Bank One, Texas, customers who do not carry a Bank One credit card, to start the process of reclaiming that business in our customers. Credit cards are a mainstream business for us. In 1966, we were the first company to offer credit cards outside California, the introduction of what is now the Visa card. Our affiliation with Merrill Lynch in 1976, introducing Merrill's cash management account, helped us to build a processing business in which we handle 3.5 million cards for third parties nationwide and 3.2 million of our own cards.

Fourth, the new competition among Texas banks for deposits will bring in new products and stimulate deposit growth. Texas already has the third-largest deposit market in the United States. We believe the new competition in the retail market will enlarge that deposit base, revitalize financial institutions seeking to build their franchise and introduce an array of deposit products that will stimulate deposit growth. We will be bringing the best products we have to market in Texas, based on our experience in five other states, including products that offer a combination of rates on packages encompassing checking accounts, certificates of deposit and automobile loans. That product experience in other states, incidentally, has been a good source of our discipline for our marketing.

Acquiring the former MCorp franchise will also give Bank One, Texas, substantial capability in commercial banking in Texas. I mention three areas among several where we will put this capability to work—all areas that we believe will stimulate both our growth and the growth of the Texas economy. The first is middle-market lending, a traditional core of strength in the MCorp organization. Countless studies have shown that middle-market companies are the job engine of the economy, creating jobs at their inception and throughout the upward course of their growth curve. The increasing diversification of the Texas economy and growth of the service and technological sectors promises to enlarge this market rapidly.

Second, we will target the competitive and very vital corporate cash-management market in Texas. The Bank One organization will acquire an excellent capability in corporate cash management and will aggressively pursue this growing market.

Finally, Bank One, Texas, will be active in energy lending, which will renew itself as the energy price cycle changes. As in-market lenders, we have avoided going outside the areas of our operations and, more important, beyond our capabilities. The Bank One, Texas, organization has an outstanding energy group, and we will be active in this market.

In closing, let me just say that if competition is a builder and a revitalizer, as I believe it is, then Texas banking and the Texas economy will benefit greatly from the new kids on the block—the fresh competition represented by the newcomers, such as ourselves. We are ready to go and eager to make a contribution in this market. We see, as others do, an opportunity to be part of a dynamic transition of the Texas banking environment and the Texas economy. The demographics are here: people in growing numbers, great resources and energy, a tradition of winning and a love of victory. Bank One, Texas, is proud to be a part of it.

Meeting the Challenges in Education

"...education is an economic issue."
—William H. Wallace

"If you go to a system where students get to choose their schools, where schools have to compete for the support of parents and students, the authority to run the schools will be decentralized.... The students will be better matched to the kinds of schools that excite them, and educational performance will improve."
—John E. Chubb

"We cannot identify characteristics of teachers and classrooms that can be used to improve the quality of schools."
—Eric A. Hanushek

"The choice issue is, I believe, one of the most powerful motivators for change available to us today."
—Milton Goldberg

"The greatest legacy we can leave to the people who will live in Texas in the 21st century is the strength of a well-educated population."
—Paul F. Roth

Introductory Remarks— Meeting the Challenges in Education

William H. Wallace

A s we look at the economy in the Southwest, we confront such issues as the competitiveness of our economy in the years ahead and the urgent question of what we need to do today to prepare our human resources to meet future needs. We face the prospect, indeed the reality, of an unprepared labor force. So, I am very happy that we have included the subject of education on the agenda for this conference. This is an economic conference, but education is an economic issue.

Various leaders in business, government and academics have been calling attention to the dilemma in education in the United States, and they are being heard. The concern about education as an issue of national priority is growing, and the connection that it has to our future economic progress is gradually being understood and gradually being brought home to the average citizen.

In September 1989 in Charlottesville, Va., at the historic home of Thomas Jefferson, the president of the United States convened an education summit involving all the nation's governors. It was a historic event. Many of the issues we will address at this conference were on the agenda of that summit meeting.

This session is titled "Meeting the Challenges in Education." These challenges are numerous, and I would like to try to structure our discussion a little bit but not to oversimplify it. They say that there are two kinds of people: those who divide everything into two kinds and those who do not. I guess I am in the former category because it seems to me that in the broadest sense there are two kinds of challenges in public education today: (1) the need to keep students in school, which is a critical concern, and (2) the need to provide a quality education for those who remain in school.

The first of these areas entails tackling the problem of the dropout rate and all of its attendant causes and ramifications. Many causes underlying the dropout rate are not direct education issues, such as broken homes, drug problems and other social issues that transcend education. Kids also drop out of school for personal reasons, such as their inability to learn or their inability to see the relevance of what they are learning to their own futures.

The second area of need is broadly defined as the quality issue. It deals with the matter of setting appropriate standards and finding means of teaching that will achieve those standards. It gets us into such questions as freedom-of-choice plans, requirements for teachers, alternative certification of teachers and how you measure achievement.

What is the role of the business community in meeting this set of educational challenges? Again, I think there are two general approaches. One is a supportive approach, which involves working through the educational systems that exist. Many good programs work today in this arena, including volunteer efforts such as Communities in Schools, the "I Have a Dream" program and other similar mentoring programs. Business is doing a lot in this area and doing it well. But the question is, Is that enough? I would say no; it is not enough.

The second approach is to lead the charge for reform. This approach is more radical, and increasingly, business leaders are becoming involved in it. Business leaders such as David Kearns, chairman of Xerox; Brad Butler, retired chairman of Procter and Gamble; and others of their stature in the business world are indicating a growing impatience because they see very clearly the critical needs of their businesses for a quality product to meet their own human resource requirements.

We have seen radical change in several areas around the country. We have seen radical change in Chicago, where the management authority in the school system has been given to neighborhood boards comprised of parents, teachers and citizens. In effect, they have taken control away from the centralized school district authority. We have seen radical changes in places like Chelsea, Mass., where under contract Boston University has assumed total control of the Chelsea School System and is running it for them. These examples are experimental, obviously, and I think it is too early to tell how they are going to work, but they are good examples of radical change.

Is either of these approaches the right way to meet the challenges that exist in education? To begin to answer this question, we need to identify those challenges and determine priorities, then we can talk more intelligently about what we need to do to meet them.

The Case for Educational Choice

John E. Chubb

I want to keep my remarks focused on what I believe is the single most promising approach to school reform that is available to us today. This is the approach to school reform that is generally known as *educational choice*. This is the approach to school reform that the Bush administration made the cornerstone of its reform efforts launched at the education summit in September 1989. It is the approach to school reform that is now on the agendas of at least 20 state legislatures around the country. It is an approach to reform that has been used with great success in several places around the country— places with very difficult populations, such as East Harlem, N.Y., and Cambridge, Mass. And it is in place statewide in several states, including Arkansas, which is one of your neighbors.

What I would like to do here is to make a case for educational choice and explain to you why I think it is the single most promising approach to educational improvement that we have available to us today. Let me begin by observing something that you will probably hear in one way or another from all the speakers, but I like to put a somewhat different twist on it. It is customary for all of us to begin talking about education today by emphasizing that we have a very serious problem, and in fact we do have a very serious problem.

Our performance, judged by just about any measure you would like to choose, has been decreasing over time, and it is bad by just about any objective standard. Our performance compares very, very unfavorably to all the nations that we consider our economic competitors. I will not go into great detail, but to give you some examples, our decline in education is not concentrated among our minority population or among our disadvantaged population. Scholastic Aptitude Test (SAT) scores, the most widely cited indicator of academic performance and the measure that is best understood by the general population, are down about 75 points over the last 20 years. SAT tests are not taken by our most disadvantaged population. Other test scores indicate basically the same thing. Dropout rates not only are high at 25 percent, but they also have scarcely improved at all over the past 20 years. In other words, they are stagnating.

In virtually every comparison of this country's students and students from other countries, especially in math and science, this country does not place third or fourth or anything like that. It is not in the middle of the pack. It comes in dead last. Most comparisons of, say, a dozen industrial nations find us in last place. This is true not only in comparison to Japan and Germany but also to the countries that are developing, such as Taiwan and Korea. So, we are just not doing very well.

But what I really want to draw attention to and what I think makes the problem especially serious is that this sad performance exists despite vigorous efforts by this country over the past 30 years to try to improve performance. For those of you who have had a decent history course or who can think back to 1957 when the Russians launched Sputnik, this country experienced a panic that we were not going to be able to keep up with the Soviets, that our educational system had fallen behind and that we needed aggressive efforts in math, science and technology. Congress passed the National Defense Education Act, and the country began aggressively introducing new approaches to math and science. There was a fever for improving the schools in the late 1950s and early 1960s. What did we get out of it? Very little.

In the mid-1960s, we discovered that our poor, our minorities, our educationally disadvantaged were in desperate shape educationally, and so we began a War on Poverty. One of the keystones of the War on Poverty was an effort to improve the education of the poor. And what do we have today? Horror stories of the education of the poor.

In 1983, Ronald Reagan unveiled the results of the National Commission on Excellence in Education's report, *A Nation at Risk*, which sent shock waves around the country that we needed to do something to improve our schools. And throughout the country, more and more money was spent on the schools. Teacher salaries were raised. Standards were increased for teachers. Standards were increased for students. Tests were given to teachers. Tests were given to students. We cracked down on student underachievement.

Let me just make this quantitative for a moment. Per-pupil educational spending in this country has increased nearly 100 percent in the last 20 years. We are spending a lot more money. Class sizes are down 25 percent. But despite all this well-meaning effort, which is often the result of the business community, educational community, politicians, civic leaders and everybody else's coming together to try to turn things around time and time again, we have not turned things around. Now we have had the education summit. Our attention is focused once again on turning things around. But what are the prospects of our really turning it around this time? Why is time number four or time number five—however you want to count it—going to be different?

Well, I believe that unless we approach our problems with a fundamentally different strategy, things are going to be fundamentally the same. After 25 or 30 years of trying to jumpstart this educational system to improve it and failing, you have to at least entertain the possibility that reform has been on the wrong track, that we have been going about it in a fundamentally wrong way.

One of the important reasons to believe that educational choice will not just bring us more of the same thing is that it is a fundamentally different way of approaching educational problems. Essentially, it says this: There are two ways that the government can provide this country with services. One is to provide those services itself, and that is what the government has been doing with education for the last 150 years or so. The alternative to that is for the government to establish a market and allow the market to provide education for the government according to the rules that the government sets down.

Educational choice represents that second approach to school improvement. Students choose the schools that they want to attend; schools compete for the support of students and parents. The marketplace sorts the good and the bad, and improvement results from that process. Now, many of you will say, "Wait a minute, wait a minute. Education is different; education is not like selling soap or oil or what have you. It is a different product. Markets are appropriate for some things; markets may not be appropriate for education."

I admit that there are several reasons to believe that education may not be an ideal product to be handled by the market. But I think that belief is, in fact, basically wrong. Let me explain briefly why I think that a market approach—a choice approach—to education makes sense. I would like to begin by presenting three simple findings of a major piece of research that we have just finished at the Brookings Institution. It is an analysis of 500 high schools nationwide, a random sample of high schools from around the country. Four hundred of them are public high schools; 100 of them are private high schools. In these high schools, we tested and studied 10,000 students and 10,000 teachers and principals. As a result of that study, we reached three empirical findings.

The first finding is that when you take everything into account—the backgrounds of kids, the backgrounds of parents, all these background circumstances—we get a fairly good picture of what good schools look like. It has very little to do with how much they are spending, their graduation requirements, their testing standards, or the size of their classes. In other words, the differences between good and bad schools, in fact, have precious little to do with many of the things that reformers have been trying to manipulate to improve schools.

Good schools, when you get right down to it, are different in ways that are hard to quantify. Good schools are different because they have fundamentally different organizations. Let me give you some examples. Good schools have ambitious, clear goals. They have a particular purpose that they are trying to accomplish. Some of you who have experience in educational matters have heard of magnet schools. Magnet schools are schools that, among other things, have a clear purpose. There are magnet schools emphasizing math and science; others emphasize computers or the performing arts. All of them bring together teachers, students, principals and staff who have a passion for a particular kind of education. It turns out that good schools, wherever they are, have the same kind of focus.

Another quality of good schools is strong leadership. They have principals who really care about education, who are focused on the school rather than being what you might call middle managers or bureaucrats who are always looking up the rules and regulations above them instead of what is happening in the school.

The final attribute of good schools is really professional teachers. They have teachers who can be trusted to make decisions, who can be involved in school decision-making processes, who have the freedom to exercise their professional judgment within their classroom to tailor education to the particular needs of their students. Students today and students tomorrow are increasingly diverse. They are demographically diverse. They have very different needs. It is very hard for a state legislature to decide how those needs should be met. The teachers have to make those decisions.

So, the first thing that we found is that good schools have very different kinds of organizations. Some of you may be familiar with a book about what sets good corporations apart from bad corporations, a book called *In Search of Excellence*. At good corporations, you find a tremendous sense of teamwork and *esprit de corps*. This is also true of good schools.

The second thing I want to stress is that, when we looked nationwide, the crucial ingredient that determined whether schools had these types of organizations was their freedom from external control by bureaucratic rules and regulations. The more heavily schools were regulated by superintendents, state legislatures, unions—the more their personnel and curriculum were constrained by bureaucratic regulation from the outside—the less likely they were to develop strong leadership or true professionalism.

Just think about it. How can you have a strongly led, professional organization when everything you are doing in that organization is being dictated to you? How, as a principal, can you put together a team of people whom you trust and respect if you do not get to say who is teaching in the school and who is not teaching in the school? If you have no control over personnel, obviously, you cannot. Bureaucracy is deadly to effective schools.

The final thing that we found, and this is the real clincher, is that when you look at public schools around the country today, only under very special circumstances are our public school systems able to relax the bureaucracy, to encourage strong leadership, to encourage professionalism, to create the kinds of environments where schools can flourish. This is happening in homogeneous, small, relatively problem-free suburban school districts. There the schools are relatively free of bureaucracy; they are doing a pretty good job, and they are well organized. Everything is fine and good. But these are not the schools that we are especially worried about.

When you look at the rest of the schools, especially city schools—large public school systems, the school systems where so many of the poor and the disadvantaged attend—instead of autonomy being provided, bureaucracy being relaxed, educational organization and professionalism flourishing, you find a vicious circle of poor performance leading to demands for change, leading to more standards, more regulations, more constraints, demoralizing further the organization and undermining performance. The question and the challenge for school reform then is, How do you break through this vicious circle?

Within the public school systems as they now stand, you will not break through this vicious circle. Technically, it is very, very difficult to provide schools with autonomy and then to hold them accountable for their performance in a way that does not bureaucratize the system. There is no objective way to measure leadership. There is no objective way to measure professionalism and to judge good teachers and bad teachers. There are no tests that do this. Any principal can tell you who the good teachers and bad teachers are, but it is very hard to quantify. The same is true of student performance. You can test for some aspects of student achievement, but you cannot measure all the qualities you want in a well-educated mind. And if you impose too many testing regulations on schools, they will begin teaching the test. Technically, it is almost impossible through a top-down process to both provide autonomy and hold the schools accountable. They are inconsistent.

Second, politically, within the current system you will not get groups, especially teachers' organizations, to agree to expand the principal's authority—giving the principal more authority and leaving the teachers unprotected. Teachers will say, "What if these principals make bad decisions? What if they fire the wrong people? We want protection." Protection means more bureaucracy. The only way that you will get autonomy in the schools and effective organization is to move to a different system of accountability, and that is a system based on choice.

Let me use one more piece of data to illustrate how choice works and why it works. Private schools, it turns out, provide autonomy wherever they are; they eschew bureaucratic regulation wherever they are. They can be Catholic schools that are parts of large systems; they can be dealing with the most difficult kinds of minority education problems, such as the Catholic education systems do throughout the East Coast. They can have any notion about what kind of values they want to impose on the schools. But, in comparison to public schools, private schools give their schools a great latitude of freedom. Why do they do that?

Principally, they do that because of choice. In the private sector, parents are choosing schools, and schools—like it or not—are forced to compete with one another and compete with the public schools. If they do not provide schools with the freedom to make decisions for themselves, to reach out, to find out what the parents want, to tailor their programs to what the parents and the kids need, then the school is not going to make it. Central organization and bureaucracy would mean death to a private school. Parents would not stand for it. If you want to organize an effective school for parents and kids, are you going to create a large system? Are you going to force parents who are unhappy to organize a lobbying campaign with the district office or the state legislature? Of course not. You are going to decentralize. The other reason you are going to decentralize organization is because it is better for education.

So, the competitive process of private schools compels them to decentralize. It compels them to organize more effectively, and as a result they are organized more effectively. Private schools have clear goals. They have strong leaders and professional teachers—and this is the key point—without anyone organizing a reform campaign to turn them around. They did it on their own. They figured it out because the competitive process forced them. That is the essence of why choice makes sense.

If you go to a system where students get to choose their schools, where schools have to compete for the support of parents and students, the authority to run the schools will be decentralized. The schools will be encouraged to organize more effectively. The schools will also be encouraged to reach out to parents for their support in education. The students will be better matched to the kinds of schools that excite them, and educational performance will improve. If we do not go down this path, if we do not change our current path, I believe that five or 10 years from now you will return to a session like this for yet another wave of school reform, and you will wonder what happened and why we did not make any progress.

If we are going to get change in this country in this direction, the business community is crucial. Everyone who is a player in the current system is essentially a very powerful force in the politics of education policy-making. If education policy is going to move toward any kind of substantial educational reform, other players who do not have a stake in the status quo have to join in the push for change. That is the most crucial role that the business community can play—getting behind the educational choice reform efforts in this state and around the country.

Schools in the 1990s: The Opportunities and Risks Facing Texas and Other States

Eric A. Hanushek

I n October 1989, when the Texas Supreme Court unanimously struck down the state's school finance statutes in the case *Edgewood Independent School District v. Kirby*, Texas was given a marvelous opportunity. The resulting requirement that the state revisit the funding and operations of its schools permits radical changes and offers the possibility of substantially improving schooling. At the same time, it must be viewed as a high-risk situation, because the result could go in a very different direction: the state could end up with just more expensive schools that offer no improvement in student performance.

In my discussion, I want to touch on several things. First, I want to provide my perspective on the economic and educational aspects of the court decision. Second, I want to relate this directly to what we know about school performance and school policy. Finally, I want to sketch some alternatives. Because each of these topics, however, is worthy of extensive discussion, I suspect I can do little more than pique your interest.

The Court Decision

Since the late 1960s, the courts of virtually every state in the nation have addressed the issue of school funding. The central issues are the distribution of educational expenditures across local jurisdictions and the interaction of local tax bases with the ability to raise funds. These cases are argued somewhat differently across states because their legal standing depends on the separate state constitutions. The *Edgewood* decision, however, has many of the elements common to the majority of state cases.

When local school districts raise funds for schools and decide how much to spend, variations in expenditures arise. The variations come from two sources: differential ability to raise funds and different preferences for education versus other places to spend money. Some people simply argue that any differences in spending should be banned. The more common argument, however, does not fully address how much variation should be allowed but just argues that differential ability to raise money should be eliminated. (The common source of differential ability to raise money is the reliance on a local property tax.)

The positions behind these court cases can be interpreted a variety of ways. They can be thought of as educational cases that represent a desire to raise the quality of schooling in poor districts. They can be thought of as taxpayer suits, where the primary objective is to shift tax burdens to other districts. Or they can be thought of as suits designed to raise the overall level of spending on education.

The Texas Supreme Court ruling concentrated on the variations in educational expenditures, which have been large in Texas. It based its ruling on a provision in the state constitution requiring the provision of "efficient" education.

Here I have my first problem with the decision. Substantial evidence, evidence to which I will return very soon, suggests that expenditures per pupil on education is a very poor measure of educational quality. Therefore, a decision concentrating on just expenditure variations is not interpreted by me to reflect underlying concerns about the distribution of education. Moreover, to an economist, the legal decision based on efficiency is very difficult to understand because efficiency is a notion that combines ideas of both costs and performance. The mere fact that expenditures vary is not a good indication of inefficiency unless one can say something about performance.

Expenditures and Policy

I frankly have not been very interested in school finance court cases for one simple reason: there is no evidence that expenditures for schooling are related to performance of schools. Yet all school finance cases center on the distribution (and maybe causes) of expenditures.

The position I am taking is clearly a bit controversial, and it is at odds with conventional wisdom. Therefore, I should provide a few more details.

A commitment to education is usually interpreted as a willingness to spend money. There is, however, little evidence that we have not been willing to spend on schools. Chart 1 presents two bits of macro data. Over the past two decades, national figures show that *real* expenditures per pupil, that is, expenditures over and above inflation, have more than doubled. This amounts to a 3.5-percent annual growth rate. At the same time, there is substantial evidence that student performance has not risen and may in fact have declined.

Chart 1 shows Scholastic Aptitude Test (SAT) performance. While there are reasons to be cautious in the interpretation of these data, other measures of performance show much the same picture.

Better evidence, however, comes from the micro level—that is, the performance of individual students and how teachers and expenditures affect them. A vast amount of research has attempted to relate educational inputs, such as characteristics of teachers and students' family backgrounds, to students' performance. I have recently attempted to compile the results of these various studies. While the details will take us a bit far afield, I should identify the key elements of this evaluation.

The basic determinants of instructional expenditures per student are class size and teacher salaries. Teacher salaries are largely determined by teacher experience and teacher education levels. The most common studies investigate how each of these separate factors affects performance, and the results are stunning. Smaller classes are not systematically related to higher student performance. Neither are teacher education and teacher experience.

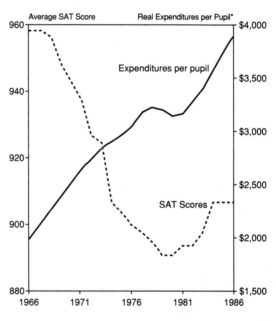

Chart 1
Real School Expenditures and
SAT Scores, 1966–86

* Current expenditures per average daily attendance (in 1985 dollars).

Moreover, if one looks farther at direct measures of expenditures or, for that matter, at a whole variety of different measures of teacher quality, one again finds no systematic relationship with performance.

The simple declarative sentence is: We cannot identify characteristics of teachers and classrooms that can be used to improve the quality of schools. There are enormous differences among teachers and schools. These differences, however, are unrelated to expenditures and simple characteristics of teachers and classroom organization.

Now let us return to the state of schools in Texas. The court order requires the state to change its financing of schools. The worst thing that could be done, in my opinion, would be to develop a system that equated expenditures across districts in the state. Taking this path would probably entail increasing the overall level of spending—something that by itself would be very wasteful. In fact, if we insist on operating the way we always have, I think that it is quite likely that changes in performance of students in Texas that result from new plans will be so small as to defy measurement.

The Alternative

I conclude from my evaluation of what we know about education that standard, input-based policies will never be very successful. State legislators or even local school boards have an extremely difficult time specifying whom to hire and how to organize schools to be effective. Moreover, just providing money within our current institutional structure will not be sufficient to improve things.

We must move to what I refer to as output-based policies. Essentially, this involves systems that reward performance.

We have evidence that we can identify good teachers. Earlier I indicated that we could not predict who would do well in the classroom. This is a very different statement. Here I am saying that we can tell after the fact who performed well. On the other hand, we have been unwilling to act on any observed differences.

A variety of alternatives fall into this category of outputs—merit pay, magnet schools, educational vouchers, tuition tax credits. They all have some common characteristics. First, they direct attention to outputs and develop mechanisms that offer some hope of redirecting resources to high performance. Second, we have virtually no experience with any of these systems. We do not know how best to implement them. We do not know how to sustain school operations with them. We do not know how to get past the huge political hurdles to even introduce them on an experimental basis.

Nonetheless, the hope for improving the quality of schools rests in moving toward such a system. Texas has an opportunity to do radical things that could change the character of schools and put Texas in a real leadership position. Alternatively, the opportunity could be lost to wrangling over a personal income tax or the like, instead of addressing educational issues head on.

Having said that, I return to a somewhat related topic that might be of particular interest to business representatives. Another aspect of schooling is the relatively small incentives for students to do well. Performance, at least for those not going to college, is never observed or used for anything important. There could be a real change if businesses routinely asked for and used transcript information. Of course, at the current time, nothing like that is really possible. Nevertheless, I offer it as an example of the kinds of changes I think we need if we are to achieve real improvements in our schools. This kind of change would have a much more powerful impact than the current business involvement.

Finally, to preempt one common reaction, I want to mention performance measurement. I do *not* believe that any system built rigidly on student test performance is appropriate. Such a system would likely have quite bad incentive properties, particularly given our current ability to construct tests. On the other hand, I do think that evaluation systems based on parental, teacher and administrator observations are possible.

American Education After A Nation at Risk

Milton Goldberg

I would like to talk briefly about a report just completed by one of our grantees, the Center for Policy Research at Rutgers University. The report, titled *The Progress of Reform: An Appraisal of State Education Initiatives*, summarizes the status of the reform activities that have occurred during the six years since the release of *A Nation at Risk*. I think it might be useful for us to catch up on the nature of these reforms, particularly the state reforms. I would also like to offer some personal views about what I believe will be the big policy questions of the 1990s—questions that groups such as this one must address.

To summarize the conclusions of this new report, state activity over the past six years has focused primarily on increasing the academic content of the curriculum and addressing the issues of teacher certification and compensation. The states have, for example, made course requirements more rigorous, increased student testing, formulated curriculum standards and, in some cases, tried to integrate the curriculum with textbooks and exams.

Let me describe one specific outcome that supports the conclusions reached by the researchers. In 1983, as we were producing *A Nation at Risk*, we studied transcripts of 1982 high school graduates. Among the 1982 high school graduates were those whose curriculum had included four years of English, three years of math, three years of science and three years of social studies—which essentially represents what we consider the core curriculum. We discovered that only about 13 percent of American high school graduates had taken such a curriculum—13 percent in 1982. The rest took courses from what *A Nation at Risk* called a "smorgasbord curriculum."

For example, in one high school we found that youngsters could select from more than 700 courses, each of which was worth as much as any other. For instance, a student could take a course in bachelor living that was worth as much as a course in biology. As a matter of fact, some of us thought that the course in bachelor living was a course in biology!

As a result of this lack of structure, more than 85 percent of American high school students in 1982 were graduating with a plethora of courses that had little meaning. So, it is no surprise to see plummeting scores on Scholastic Aptitude Tests (SATs) and other tests as well. If you do not pick the course and you do not take the work, there is a fair chance you are not going to learn the subject.

In 1987, we undertook a similar study of high school transcripts and discovered that 30 percent of American high school seniors that year were graduating with four years of English, three years of math, three years of science and three years of social studies. Apparently, in the years since *A Nation at Risk* was published, the American people had decided to adopt one of the changes recommended in that report: an increase in course-taking requirements. By 1987, almost one-third of high school graduates had taken the New Basics curriculum.

The second major change—and the second major conclusion to be drawn from the analysis of state reform done by the Center for Policy Research—is that despite national pressure for reform, the type of reform occurring in each state is essentially a reflection of the political culture of the state rather than a response to national pressure. For example, in states with a governor from one political party and a legislature controlled by another, a smorgasbord of reforms was adopted, usually as the result of either conciliation or argument and not because of a coherent policy. States with traditions of large-scale policy fixes chose to continue in that direction. States that favored incremental approaches and were used to pragmatic problem-solving went about educational reform in just that way. One of the big problems faced by a lot of states involved deciding who got the credit for reform, without concomitant regard to whether or not the reform actually resulted in improvement. Who got credit for it? Was it the legislature? Was it the governor? Or was it some other body in the state?

The third characteristic of the reform movement is that, in the main, states have tended to choose those reforms that are more easily implemented rather than adopting more complex recommendations. The most popular reform of the past five years has been increasing graduation requirements. Why? Because it is uncomplicated. All you have to do is say, "Starting next year, everybody has to take three years instead of two" of whatever subject. States have gone this route. In contrast, reforms requiring, for example, increased funding or changes in authority patterns or a complex restructuring of instruction and administration either were not passed or were lost very quickly after passage. It was the manageable, easily defined reforms that stuck.

Fourth, reforms lacked coherence. Through their adoption of frequently unrelated reforms, policymakers sent conflicting messages to teachers and administrators while failing to establish priorities. In other words, the reforms were not part of any coherent policy agreement reached at the state level about desired outputs and the inputs needed to achieve those goals.

Fifth, the easy reforms, the ones that I described as manageable, have stayed in place. Increased curricular requirements, for example, have stuck. But more complicated reforms, such as career ladders for teachers, either were never passed or were eventually rescinded. While they have lasted in some places, in the main these reforms have proven much less successful than the easier, more manageable changes.

Finally with regard to the economy—and this is as much my personal view as it is the report's view—there is some indication that the economic expansion experienced by this country in the early 1980s, even with the recession, was crucial to the reform movement. In states where more money was available, reform took off more quickly. States experiencing economic upswings were, as a matter of fact, active in reform. However, it is important to note that a substantial number of poor states initiated reforms that were, in some cases, as complicated as the reforms initiated in the economically well-off states.

Well, that is a brief summary of the conclusions of the Center's report. Now, based on that report and my own views about changes in this country since 1983, I would like to offer some thoughts on what I believe to be the important policy questions you will need to address over the next decade.

First is the complex of issues that includes site-based management, neighborhood control of schools and educational choice. These issues really have to do with deregulation of education, a subject that President George Bush has talked about a great deal. I was privileged to be at last September's historic education summit and heard a lot of conversation on this topic.

Deregulation is a very complicated business. Those people who cry out for deregulation often are disenchanted by it once that have the opportunity to practice it. Let me share with you one anecdote.

I have been associated with a project involving 16 school districts in eight different states. Launched by then Secretary of Education William J. Bennett and then Governor of Tennessee Lamar Alexander, this project involved telling the school districts in question, "You identify the regulations that get in the way of achievement in your school districts, either for teachers or for students. You tell us what the regulations are, and we, the federal government and the state governments, will figure out a way to remove the requirements." Well, let me tell you, many of those districts have had trouble identifying regulations that stand in their way.

In one case, when a district succeeded in identifying such troublesome regulations, the governor was unable to get the particular regulations waived. The district wanted to introduce early childhood education into the schools. The parents wanted it; the community wanted it. The superintendent sought to put classes for 4-year-olds into the school building. However, there is a code in that particular state specifying that you cannot hold classes for 4-year-old children unless you have a bathroom in the room. The regulation was not put in the books by educators; it was put in the books by others who had the well-being of the youngsters at heart. The fact is, though, that to comply with the code, the superintendent would have had to spend so much money on capital improvement that he could not manage it. So, he asked if he could rearrange his school organization for the children's classrooms to be opposite the bathrooms. The youngsters could walk across the hall to the bathroom. That was two years ago. The superintendent still has not been able to accomplish this. The governor is on his side, but all the regulatory problems that need to be overcome within the state bureaucracy—not just the education bureaucracy but the larger bureaucracy as well—remain.

The third policy question relates to the example I just gave you. Across the country, we are seeing a movement toward the expansion of services for young children under the age of 5 or 6. And that is not just an educational issue. It is also a social and economic issue. It has to do with the role of the family in society and the role of social agencies that are presently involved with young children. I think that in this country, we are a long way from understanding the kinds of complicated policies that need to be considered as we move very quickly toward providing more and more services for young children.

Fourth is the question of the inner cities in this country. They still present us with our most difficult educational challenges. That is not to suggest that other communities do not have problems—they do; but until we crack the problems of the big cities, I am not sure we will accomplish much more. It may be that breaking up the system as Chicago has done—it may be that creating the kind of choice that East Harlem has adopted—is the wave of the future. I would like to suggest that improving education in the inner cities must be a nationwide priority.

Educational choice can be one of the most powerful motivators for change available to us. I would therefore propose it as the fifth big policy issue. I believe that no group considering educational improvement at either the local or state level can avoid addressing educational choice.

And finally, let me voice an appeal. Education is woeful in its inability to use good information. You as business leaders should recognize that the success of business in America has been based on its ability to use good information when it is available. To the degree that you can play a role, you could demand that schools tell you why they do what they do. What is the basis for their decisions? What is the evidence that implementing a given policy will likely lead to a desired outcome? That question needs to be asked of teachers, principals, legislators, governors, commissioners of education and superintendents. All those who play a role in improving education need to be asked if they know the *bases* for their decisions.

Meeting the Challenges in Education

Paul F. Roth

I appreciate the opportunity to share some of my thoughts concerning education. To put it bluntly, Texas is in big trouble. Our state generates some $300 billion in goods and services each year, creating the 10th-largest economy in the world. Yet one out of every three Texans may not be able to read or write well enough to hold a meaningful job in our state.

This weakness was not such a crucial factor when oil and cotton fueled the Texas economy. Today, this weakness represents an economic time bomb as our ability to compete with other states and other countries for business growth and development is based more and more on knowledge.

Dr. Blake Cherrington, dean of the School of Engineering and Computer Science at the University of Texas at Dallas, says we are in a transition from an economy where we sell our natural resources to an economy where we sell our mental resources, and I am afraid our mental resources are underwhelming. We have heard the startling facts, but here is a brief recap.

- In Texas, 33 percent of all high school students drop out before graduating. By comparison, the overall U.S. dropout rate is 25 percent, and the Japanese rate is less than 10 percent.
- Ninety percent of the inmates in Texas prisons are high school dropouts.
- Texas ranks 47th among the 50 states in overall literacy.
- The estimated cost of illiteracy in Texas is $17 billion for each class of students.

Let us look at the story behind the statistics. Walk the halls of a typical high school today and what will you see? You will see a mirror image of the priorities our society has set. You will probably see a lot of kids who have invested far more time and energy playing video games than they have invested in learning to write a good, grammatically correct paragraph. You will probably see kids who can name more brands of beer than U.S. presidents. You will see kids who average three hours to five hours of television viewing per day, and you will probably see teachers who have slowly, over time, lowered their expectations and their standards because, after all, you cannot retain 50 percent or 60 percent of an entire class.

But I want to focus on solutions, not problems. The need for educational change has come about because the world has changed. Business is also under pressure to restructure in response to a rapidly changing global economy. As a result, three megatrends are redefining corporate America as we move into the 1990s.

The first megatrend is our country's changing demographics. The declining birth rate, or baby bust, will slash the number of new workers entering the labor force. This will force business to draw more and more of its entry-level recruits from a smaller segment of the population, and tomorrow's new workers will not be like today's new workers. Roughly 75 percent of the new entrants to the Texas work force between now and the end of the century will be women and minorities. Yet in our state, the Hispanic dropout rate is 45 percent, and the dropout rate for blacks is 34 percent. So, many of tomorrow's new workers may well lack basic reading, writing and reasoning skills, making that smaller segment of new workers a less prepared segment.

A second megatrend that will have an impact on the way we do business is that tomorrow's jobs are likely to require more skills, not fewer, than today's jobs. Technology is dramatically changing the business world, and technological innovation will continue to accelerate the pace of change that a successful business must go through. Workers must continually learn to do things differently and to acquire new skills.

The third megatrend that I will cite is the globalization of the economy. In the Industrial Age, the United States led the race. With our manufacturing know-how, we took our natural resources and resources from other countries and produced products that we sold to ourselves and to people around the world. That is what created our affluent middle-class lifestyle. But today, other countries produce many of those same goods for less money, and many times at a higher quality, than we can.

So as we begin the last decade of this century, the number of new workers is dropping. The composition of our work force is changing in profound ways. The basic skills of our work force are eroding at a time when more skills are required, and the United States is facing its stiffest international competition in recent memory. This is why business must become involved in education.

Business is responding. Across the state, corporations have become increasingly involved with education from participating in dropout prevention and work-study programs to recognizing outstanding teachers.

As good as these individual initiatives are, they must be part of a comprehensive, well-coordinated master plan for changing our educational system in Texas, a plan that provides for ongoing cooperation among educators, business and the community. And for the first time, we are moving in that direction.

Earlier this year, the Texas Research League sponsored a summit conference on the state of education in Texas and actions needed to steer us back on course. As a result, the Texas Chamber of Commerce established an education task force. It was my privilege to chair this group.

The task force recommended a coalition of business leaders, educators and parents to enhance the education process in our state. We are organizing the coalition now. Together we will design an educational system that meets the work force needs of business, the academic prerequisites of higher education and the general needs of society.

Business knows the talents and skills it must have to be successful in the global marketplace. Educators know how to achieve quality education if they are allowed to approach the learning process in a creative and innovative way. Parents play perhaps the most important role of all in providing guidance, support, direction and encouragement for their children.

This broad-based alliance will have the staying power and the resources to realize positive, fundamental change for public education in Texas. But change will not come overnight. It will require our long-term commitment.

Simply stated, the purpose of the business and education coalition is to achieve a dramatic increase in student achievement in Texas. We want a level of opportunity and quality of life second to none as we enter the 21st century. It is vital that we keep students in school through graduation and that they achieve the highest degree of competency.

We envision the coalition as catalyst, coordinator and communicator. We will emphasize that education is the underpinning of our society, that it is essential to a growing economy, the key to our competitiveness.

It is critical that we clearly distinguish between programs that affect long-term improvements in the education process and those that offer immediate assistance for students now in the classroom. The coalition will coordinate efforts that accomplish both.

I want to briefly outline the coalition's four priority areas. The first priority is education leadership, teaching and instruction-content issues. The coalition will develop management training programs for education leadership and incentives that promote excellence in teaching. The coalition will seek new technologies that afford customized training opportunities, increased coaching time between teacher and student and reduced administrative requirements.

Second, in the area of student issues, the coalition will identify appropriate student performance standards and measurement criteria. Then, we will provide local school boards, principals and teachers the support needed to implement those measures. The business and education coalition will promote effective programs that encourage students to remain in school.

Third, to enhance business and community support of education, the coalition will foster parental involvement in their children's education and encourage business to become a full partner with the schools by committing human and financial resources.

The coalition's fourth priority is to target regulatory and legislative issues, such as funding and school system structure. As you are aware, we are at a crossroads in public school funding in Texas today in light of the state supreme court's recent ruling. The coalition will take a position on the tough issue of equitable school district financing. We will also work to modify rules and policies that create roadblocks to improving education.

These are the coalition's four priority areas. Now let us look at its organizational structure. We see the coalition as being two-tiered. It will exist as a statewide organization for coordination and communication between local communities and consolidation of policy recommendations; at the local grassroots level, coalition members will help implement programs designed to improve education. Members will also represent their communities on statewide task forces that will be established to focus on the coalition's key priorities.

Already more than 150 companies, associations and chambers of commerce have pledged their support for the coalition, and the number grows each day. Some of the business and education communities' best and brightest are leading the process. These individuals include Bobby Inman, who earlier this morning eloquently outlined some of the challenges and opportunities we face; Jerry Junkins, chairman of Texas Instruments; Linus Wright, now a Dallas business-man and former superintendent of the Dallas Independent School District and former undersecretary of education in Washington, D.C.; Bill Stevens, president of Exxon; Jerry Carlson, vice president and general manager of IBM; Bill Kirby, commissioner of education; and Kenneth Ashworth, commissioner of higher education. Other companies heavily involved in this important initiative include USAA, Lone Star Gas, TU Electric and Southwestern Bell.

Public education in Texas is everyone's concern—businesses, educators, parents, local communities, governments—because the dimensions of the challenges we face reach across the entire spectrum of society. I believe the greatest legacy we can leave to the people who will live in Texas in the 21st century is the strength of a well-educated population.

We must work together to ensure that all our young people—as well as the businesses that ultimately will tap their talents—graduate to the promise and excitement that tomorrow should hold.

The Challenges of the International Marketplace

"Lifting the barriers to trade liberates the creative talents of people and releases the dynamic energies of entrepreneurs. Protectionism seduces, but free trade produces!"
—Carl E. Rufelds

"The Mexican government's total foreign debt exceeds half of the nation's gross domestic product."
—William C. Gruben

"Each of the Pacific Basin countries is going through industrial catch-up, and it is the United States that is being caught."
—Lawrence B. Krause

The Canada–U.S. Free Trade Agreement: A New Reality, A New Challenge

Carl E. Rufelds

I am very pleased to be in such distinguished company on this afternoon's panel to talk to you about the challenges of the international marketplace, and specifically about the challenges that lie ahead after the first 10 months of the operation of the Canada–U.S. Free Trade Agreement (FTA), an agreement that will indeed make the 1990s a different decade in Canada–U.S. trade relations.

It is timely that I speak to you about the new reality of the FTA because the agreement is still in its infancy. It is a vigorous sprout, but it is still too young to fend entirely for itself. It requires careful nurturing at the political level while it is testing its legs at the private level. That is the challenge I want to focus on today—the challenge of making the agreement work for the benefit of both countries, and in particular for the Southwest economy.

In these protectionist times, the term *free trade* has become one of the more abused phrases of our common language. On the lips of some, it is pronounced in evangelical tones. On the lips of others, it has a more doubtful ring. All too often both believers and doubters qualify the phrase so that it becomes *free and fair trade*. Translated, this all too often means free, fair and *managed* trade.

The agreement promises great benefits, but we have to work hard to realize them. It was, after all, hard work and political courage and vision that brought us the FTA in the first place. So, let me spend a few moments recalling the circumstances that led Canada and the United States to seek this new trading relationship.

The origin of the free trade negotiations lay in a broadly shared consensus among political and economic circles in both countries that the time had come to find a new approach, a new blueprint for trade between Canada and the United States. By themselves, the facts and figures of our bilateral trade provide eloquent testimony in support of a trade agreement tailored to our unique circumstances.

Canada and the United States enjoy the largest trading relationship of any two countries in the world. In 1988, cross-border trade in goods and services exceeded $176 billion. As a matter of comparison, the budget of the Canadian federal government was $111 billion. The U.S. market accounts for about 75 percent of all Canadian exports. The Canadian market, on the other hand, accounts for almost 25 percent of all U.S. exports—about double the U.S. exports to Japan and almost equal to U.S. exports to all 12 countries of the European Community. In fact, U.S. merchandise exports to Canada in 1988 were equal to the total of U.S. exports to some 101 countries around the world.

On the investment side, more than 72 percent of Canadian direct foreign investment was in the United States in 1987. Looking the other way, Canada received more U.S. investment than any other country, more than 18 percent of U.S. direct investment abroad in 1987.

So, the numbers were very big and the stakes were very high for both countries when we came to negotiate the Free Trade Agreement. The stakes remain very high today as we implement the agreement. The stakes may be higher for Canada because we are more dependent on the relationship in terms of immediate interests. But the risks may be greater for the United States in terms of both immediate and long-range interests.

Our old trading arrangement, the Geneva-based General Agreement on Tariffs and Trade (GATT), has served us well. But the rules of GATT were no longer adequate. Moreover, they were not evolving fast enough to restrain the resurgent forces of protectionism or to come to grips with the dynamics of the new international trading environment, new competitors and new technologies. Put another way, Canada–U.S. trade is too large and too complex to fit comfortably within the old suit of clothes that GATT provided. In the mid-1980s, the stresses and strains on the fabric were apparent. Trade relations between Canada and the United States were characterized by increasing tensions and growing frustrations. The number and gravity of our problems seemed to be rising in inverse proportion to our capacity to find solutions to them.

We needed something new to shore up the foundations and provide a new design for growth. We needed to resume control of our own trading relationship, to get away from the lowest common denominator, to go further and faster than the rest of the world appeared to be willing to go.

Well, we succeeded. While everybody else talked about free trade, we did something about it. Negotiations began in the spring of 1986 and concluded in the fall of 1987. The agreement was signed on Jan. 1, 1988. It was brought into force on Jan. 1, 1989.

Once again, Canada and the United States made history together. The Free Trade Agreement is the largest, most comprehensive bilateral trade agreement ever known. And it is fully consistent with GATT. The agreement covers more ground than the original Treaty of Rome that established the European Community comprised of six member countries. Indeed, it encompasses a $5 trillion North American economy that is 15-percent larger than the economy of today's European Community comprised of 12 member countries.

All tariffs on Canada–U.S. trade will soon be gone. Many have already been eliminated. Others will disappear faster than planned because the agreement has already whetted the appetite of industry on both sides of the border for a more rapid pace of tariff elimination.

The principle of nondiscrimination has been brought to bear on our cross-border trade in services and our cross-border investments. Business travel across the border has been facilitated. The rule of law has been brought to the settlement of disputes. New procedures have been introduced to help avoid disputes in the first instance. New institutions have been created to oversee the implementation of the agreement and assure its further growth.

We have succeeded, indeed, as no two other trading partners have ever done before. But we should realize that the success of the free trade negotiations could possibly mean the failure of the Free Trade Agreement if we believe that our work is complete.

What I am saying is that FTA is a means to an end, not an end in itself. The end is the liberalization of trade and investment in a climate of greater stability and predictability. The end is growth and mutual prosperity. The end is also a strong bilateral model for a more open multilateral trading system.

The Free Trade Agreement represents a giant step toward the achievement of these ends. But we must not forget the obstacle course we had to face in taking that step. If we are to make the agreement itself a success, we need to remember every rock and every bump and every pothole along the road. We need to remember the political capital that we have invested in coming as far as we have come. And we need to remember that we have not yet made it all the way home.

In the United States, the free trade negotiations were conducted against the background of a rising tide of protectionism. It was a tough fight, and more than once the negotiators were almost knocked out of the ring. In the end, political leadership and, yes, political courage prevailed and allowed the national interest to overcome special interests.

Today, there are still voices in the United States that call for protectionist measures in one form or another. President George Bush has warned against the "fool's gold" of protectionism, but talk continues on Capitol Hill and in business circles about managed trade, with imports and exports fixed by quotas.

Frustration with Japan continues to mount. Hopes for Europe 1992 are overladen with fears of new restrictions. Itchy trigger fingers are poised over the arsenal of trade weapons provided by last year's omnibus Trade and Competitiveness Act.

In Canada, too, we had to put up a tough fight for FTA in the face of heavy domestic opposition. But our fight went far deeper than yours. While the United States debated the economic benefits of the agreement, Canadians debated the nature and future of their country and the nature and future of its relationship with the United States. Emotions ran high, and divisions ran deep.

The Canadian debate culminated in the election that returned Prime Minister Brian Mulroney's government to office in November 1988. In the end, the debate provided catharsis. Political courage and conviction carried the day, and Canada voted for the future rather than the status quo.

But today, there are still voices in Canada that decry the Free Trade Agreement and blame it for all the country's real or imagined ills. Every corporate merger, every plant closure, every measure to fight our budget deficit—all these and more are ascribed to the Free Trade Agreement, whereas the success stories, the new investments, the plant expansions gain little notice.

My point, again, is that we must not rest on our laurels. We all know that any athlete who skips practice to read his or her press clippings will soon have no clippings to read. The voice of reason won the debates in both countries in 1988. But the forces that almost defeated the agreement will be with us through the 1990s as we face the task of implementation.

Having sounded this cautionary note, I am particularly pleased to report that we have made a good start in the implementation process—in practical, institutional and political terms. In practical terms, the first tariff cuts automatically came into effect on Jan. 1, 1989. A new system of certifying the Canadian or U.S. origin of goods for tariff purposes has also come into effect without any serious difficulty.

Indeed, as I have already suggested, this part of the agreement is working so well that businesses on both sides of the border are lining up to press their claims for a speedier reduction of tariffs. This is a very promising development because it shows that companies are positioning themselves to exploit the advantages of the agreement. With requests covering more than 2,000 items already filed by both the United States and Canada, a joint working group is being created to develop a mutually beneficial package of accelerated tariff cuts by Jan. 1, 1990. We hope that the initiative shown by industry in respect to tariffs will be shown in other areas as well.

In institutional terms, the implementation of the agreement received a solid boost with the first meeting of the new Canada–U.S. Trade Commission, held in Washington, D.C., on March 13, 1989. Trade Minister John Crosbie and U.S. Trade Representative Carla Hills concurred that the commission would be the central implementing body for the agreement and the principal channel for the two parties to deal with each other on bilateral trade matters. The commission will meet at least twice a year for these purposes.

Fleshing out certain important institutional provisions of the agreement, the commission created eight working groups to attempt to reduce trade barriers that arise from differing standards and approaches in such areas as rules of origin, automotive issues, unfair trade practices and trade remedy laws. So, all systems are go in institutional terms. The commission has taken charge. The working groups are getting down to business or are about to do so.

In political terms, Prime Minister Mulroney and President Bush declared their commitment to the effective implementation of the agreement in Ottawa in February 1988 and again in Maine in the summer of 1989. They made it clear that the agreement must make a real difference and must be seen to be making a real difference in our trade relations. They concurred that the implementation requires political oversight and nurturing in its early stages.

Sustained political oversight will help us to avoid problems in the first place. Sustained political oversight will help us to resolve the problems that cannot be avoided, to resolve them by compromise or by reference to dispute-settlement procedures, as appropriate. Sustained political oversight calls for both governments to avoid narrow and legalistic approaches, to look beyond the letter of the text and to reinforce the spirit of the agreement. Deeds must follow words, and the 1990s will be the time for deeds—deeds by governments to give the most expansive and constructive effect to the obligations they accepted in entering into the Free Trade Agreement and deeds by the private sector to exploit the new opportunities for increased trade, investment and job creation. The opportunities are there. Look at the Southwest, for instance.

In 1988, sales of Southwest-made (including Texas, Oklahoma, New Mexico, Kansas, Louisiana and Arkansas) goods to Canada totaled more than $4.3 billion. At the same time, Canada exported more than $2.6 billion in goods to the Southwest, giving this region a favorable trade balance with Canada of $1.7 billion. (To put that in context, the total U.S. imbalance of trade with Korea is approximately $2 billion, so the Southwest is doing its share to reduce the U.S. trade imbalance in total.) And these numbers do not reflect trade that did not occur because of high tariffs or nontariff barriers that were in place before the Free Trade Agreement took effect.

What can we expect in the future for the Southwest and the Free Trade Agreement? The FTA changes the fundamental rules of the game for Canada–Southwest U.S. trade. Let me illustrate with a few examples. The agreement unshackles our trade from tariffs. In national terms, tariff elimination, when it is completed, will mean a savings of $1.7 billion a year for U.S. exporters relative to 1987 trade. With every year that trade increases, the savings will increase. To illustrate my point about the savings resulting from the elimination of tariffs under the FTA, let us look at the impact on Texas and a couple of its major exports to Canada. Computer exports from Texas to Canada topped $172 million in 1988. On Jan. 1, 1989, the Canadian tariff of 3.9 percent was eliminated, adding almost $7 million per year to the bottom line of Texas exporters of computers to Canada. Exports of organic chemicals from Texas were almost $201 million in 1988, and Canadian tariffs, some as high as 10 percent, will be phased out over five years, yielding further savings to state exporters.

Think of tariff elimination as a reverse tax, payable on delivery or, better still, as a fund that companies here can use to compete against Japanese, Korean, European and other foreign suppliers in the Canadian market.

On another front of importance to the Southwest, the agreement locks in the rules of the game for energy. Producers and consumers in the United States and Canada can plan investments and make decisions about types of fuel use more easily, knowing that the regulatory framework in both countries will be fairly and openly administered and that there will be security of supply and market.

Moreover, in general economic terms, since 1982 Canada's gross domestic product (GDP) has grown by an average of 4.3 percent per year, equaling Japan's GDP, which is at the head of the Group of Seven (G–7) industrialized countries. So, Canada's general economic growth, spurred further by the FTA, will continue to mean that it is a good market for investment and products from the Southwest. We are confident that the FTA will work and that substantial new benefits will be realized.

But, we also know that protectionism is not dead. We know that our two countries continue to have differences on plywood, wool, pork and Pacific salmon and herring, to list only a few. These difficulties, however, cannot obscure the new reality of the Free Trade Agreement. They are part of the challenge of implementing the agreement and must not be blown out of proportion. In both Canada and the United States, we are confident that we can meet the challenge of implementation. Our confidence is born from the vitality of the institutions and the strength of the rules created under the Free Trade Agreement. Our confidence is born of the knowledge that the agreement gives both our countries an added stake in each other's future and fortune. And our confidence is born of the empirical experience of trade liberalization over the past 40 years. Lifting the barriers to trade liberates the creative talents of people and releases the dynamic energies of entrepreneurs. Protectionism seduces, but free trade produces!

Both governments are committed to the agreement and to providing the executive oversight and management necessary to make it work. Both governments recognize that successful implementation is crucial not only to the bilateral relationship but also to negotiating better market access and improved international trading rules with Japan, Europe and the developing countries.

From time to time, we Canadians may have to remind you that we are the ones you have an agreement with, not Europe or Japan. But in the end, together, we will make the agreement work. We will make this new reality in law a new reality in fact.

The Mexican Economy

William C. Gruben

M exico's economy is showing signs of turning the corner, but it still faces many problems. I will discuss the positive signs and address the problems.

Despite its problems, the Mexican economy has grown in 1989. Both capital goods and consumer goods show output growth in 1989 (Chart 1). This growth is in marked contrast to 1986, when a major decline in oil prices sent the nation's economy into a tailspin.

Furthermore, despite sluggishness in its important oil industry, Mexico's overall exports are growing. For the first five months of 1989, for example, exports were up 5 percent from a year earlier. Chart 2 depicts components of Mexico's overall exports, expressed in dollars. Mexico's exports are rising because the manufacturing sector is taking up the slack left by the energy sector.

Mexico has been expanding capacity as well. Chart 3 shows rates of change in investment in Mexico. It suggests that expectations of further growth have become more optimistic in the last couple of years, after serious problems in the mid-1980s. After a major decline in 1986, investment began to grow in 1987 and continued to grow in 1988.

To attract still more investment and to create more jobs, Mexico is now taking additional steps to attract foreign investors. Aside from the *maquiladoras* (the in-bond export factories that allow 100-percent foreign ownership), most types of manufacturing and other firms in Mexico have been required to have Mexican-majority ownership. Mexico has liberalized its ownership requirements and opened ownership of many new types

Chart 1
Industrial Production

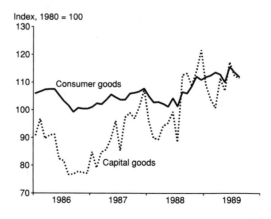

Index, 1980 = 100

Chart 2
Foreign Currency Revenues from Exports

Chart 3
Growth in Real Private-Sector Investment

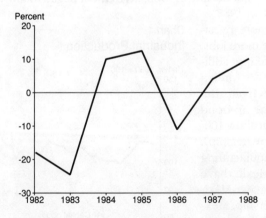

of firms to foreign investors. Table 1 shows industries in which firms may be 100-percent owned by foreign investors.

Mexico has also taken steps to make the country more economically efficient. The Mexican government has sold or closed hundreds of state-owned enterprises, from airlines to steel mills and hotels (Chart 4). These money-losing enterprises have been a significant drain on the government's scarce resources. In another move toward efficiency, Mexico has also liberalized its import policies, partly in an attempt to introduce sufficient competition to hold down domestic prices.

Table 1
Industries in Mexico that Allow 100-Percent Foreign Ownership

• Food, beverages and tobacco
• Textiles, apparel and leather
• Lumber and paper
• Chemicals (except oil refining and basic secondary petrochemicals)
• Machinery (except firearms and ammunition)
• Other manufacturing industries (except mining)
• Restaurants, hotels and commerce (except liquified gas, firearms and ammunition)

Moreover, Mexico has pursued an austerity program (Table 2). Wage and price controls have been imposed. And in an effort to provide a sense of stability and to hold back any inflationary effects of major devaluation, Mexico has instituted a controlled exchange-rate slide of one peso per day against the U.S. dollar.

Table 2
Mexico's Austerity Program

• Price Controls
• Wage Controls
• Intervention in the foreign-exchange market

Mexico has worked hard to lower its inflation rate. It imposed the austerity program and absolute reductions in the monetary base. It has liberalized import policies. Chart 5 presents annualized rates of Mexican inflation and shows that Mexico's protracted period of hyperinflation is over.

In sum, Mexico is showing positive signs. Output is growing. Inflation is declining. Investment is picking up. The Mexican government has taken steps to reduce restrictions on the private sector and to increase competition within the country. But Mexico still has problems as well. Some problems are well known, and others are a little less obvious.

Chart 4
Mexican Government-Owned Enterprises

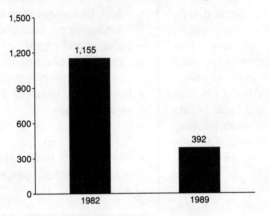

Chart 5
Mexican Annualized Rate of Inflation

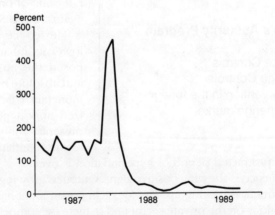

Mexico's most well-known current problem is its foreign debt. Mexico's external public debt is now about $100 billion—a serious problem. Indeed, as Chart 6 shows, the Mexican government's total foreign debt exceeds half of the nation's gross domestic product. As a portion of gross domestic product, the debt is falling. Nevertheless, payments on this debt represent a major financial drain on the nation's economy.

Chart 6
Foreign Debt as a Percentage of Gross Domestic Product

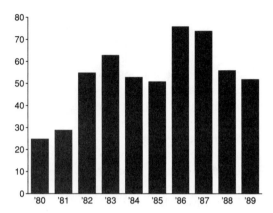

But foreign debt is only one of Mexico's difficulties. Mexico's deficits have resulted in a significant run-up in its domestic debt. Chart 7 depicts the dollar value of Mexico's public domestic debt. The Mexican government is using this money to fund both internal deficits and hard-currency liabilities.

One problem with these debt levels is that the Mexican public sector has sopped up savings that are needed to expand both private and public productive capacity in the country. Chart 8 shows Mexico's levels of private and public investment as a percentage of its gross domestic product. These proportions compare with about 30 percent in some of the rapidly growing, newly industrialized Pacific nations. Mexico simply is not getting enough capital to make the investment efforts needed to stay competitive with those countries. It is increasingly evident that some of Mexico's public infrastructure is deteriorating. Mexico City's water system, for example, loses about 30 percent of its water through leaky pipes and other

Chart 7
Mexican Public-Sector Domestic Debt

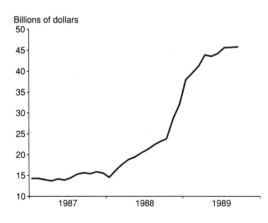

weaknesses in the system. This compares with about 15 percent in the United States and 12 percent in Europe. And because of past low levels of investment, Mexico has a great deal of catching up to do.

It is for these reasons that Mexico's programs to make its economy more efficient and its public sector less burdensome, such as selling off inefficient state-owned government enterprises, are so important. Likewise, it is for these reasons that Mexico hopes that these stabilizing

Chart 8
Mexican Private- and Public-Sector Investment

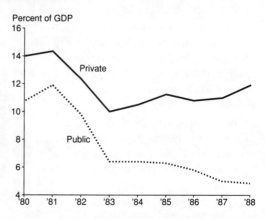

measures will attract Mexican flight capital back to the country to facilitate further investment. To some extent, this strategy appears to have started to work. Chart 9 shows the levels of total Mexican private (or nongovernmental) deposits in U.S. banks. They have lately begun to fall, suggesting that some repatriation of Mexican capital is occurring. But as Chart 8 (on investment) suggests, it has not been enough so far.

Another sign of capital shortages in Mexico is the interest rate the Mexican government must pay on its short-term domestic debt. Chart 10 shows interest

Chart 9
Mexican Private Deposits in the U.S.

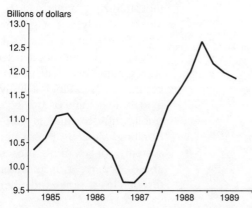

rates on Mexican one-month treasury bills. With the dramatic decline in Mexico's inflation rate, the rates Mexico has lately had to pay to get needed domestic capital have been falling markedly. This is good. But it is also important to note that Mexico's inflation rate in August 1989 was 1 percent per month, or an annual rate of about 13 percent. At the same time, Mexican treasury-bill rates were about 34 percent. This means a real rate, or inflation-adjusted rate, of about 21 percent, which is very high and suggests continued problems of capital shortage.

In an attempt to alleviate Mexico's debt and capital-shortage problems, U.S. Treasury Secretary Nicholas Brady offered a plan (Table 3). A principal purpose of the Brady Plan is to encourage new loans to Mexico. U.S. banks have three options under this plan. The first is designed to address Mexico's capital-shortage problems. Banks choosing this option can issue new loans to-

---

Table 3
The Brady Plan's Three Options

- Issue new loans totaling 25 percent of current exposure. No charge against bonds.
- Swap existing loans for market-rate bonds. Bonds are discounted 35 percent from face value of the loan amount.
- Swap existing loans for 6.25-percent bonds valued at the face value of the loan amount.

---

taling 25 percent of their current loan exposure. The other two options do not involve new loans. The second option provides for swapping existing loans for bonds that trade at market rates. But the bonds will be discounted 35 percent from the face value of the loan amount. The third option also involves a loan-for-a-bond swap. In this case, the bonds are valued at the face value of the loans, but there is a penalty. The interest rate on the bonds is only 6.25 percent. Thus, the Brady Plan offers banks the opportunity to stay in the Mexican lending market or to get out, but at a cost.

But recent announcements by some large U.S. lenders suggest problems for the goals of the Brady Plan. In September 1989, Chase Manhattan boosted its loan-loss reserves for developed-country loans by $1.15 billion. A few days earlier, Manufacturers Hanover had announced that it was raising loan-loss reserves for less-developed-country loans. These steps suggest that two of the largest lenders to Mex-

Chart 10
Interest Rate on Mexican One-Month Treasury Bills

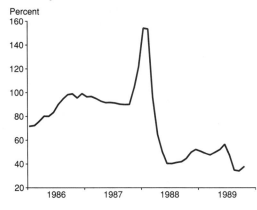

Percent

ico will not be participating in the first option of the Brady Plan. They will not continue to lend to Mexico. Indeed, so far, Citibank is the only major U.S. financial institution that has publicly committed itself to continue operations in the Mexican market.

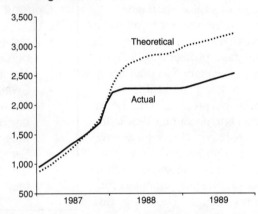

Chart 11
Actual and Theoretical Peso–Dollar Exchange Rates

We have looked at Mexico's debt problem and its implications, but that is not the only possible problem. I noted that one component of Mexico's austerity program is the controlled exchange-rate slide. Mexico is allowing the peso to slide against the dollar at a rate of one peso per day. That is, according to this controlled slide, Mexicans have to pay one more peso per dollar every day. This step represents an attempt to avoid the inflationary problems that a devaluation can induce. It is also an attempt to avoid the investor uncertainty that a major devaluation can generate: When one major devaluation occurs, investors may begin to worry about the possibility of another. This uncertainty would interfere with Mexico's program to repatriate capital that Mexicans have shipped overseas. As Chart 11 suggests, this part of the austerity program may have trouble. Chart 11 shows the difference between the actual peso–dollar exchange rates and the rates they would likely be if they were allowed to fluctuate freely. The actual rate is labeled *actual.* The rate they would probably be if rates could fluctuate freely is labeled *theoretical.* The chart suggests that the number of pesos per dollar would have to increase by more than 25 percent to reach a free-market rate.

Chart 12 gives us an idea of why this difference between actual and probable free-market rates exists. It shows changes in Mexican foreign currency reserves. These reserves fell from about $16 billion at the end of 1987 to a little more than $6.5 billion a year later—a decline of more than one-half. They declined by another $500 million in the first quarter of 1989. This means that the reserves Mexico uses to control the slide of the peso are diminishing rapidly. Furthermore, while Mexico has greatly reduced its inflation rate, it would take more than two years of one-peso-per-day slides in the exchange rate to bring the exchange rate back to what the market would probably dictate. But there is reason to believe that Mexico's inflation rate may exceed the U.S. rate in the future. First, the wage–price controls and the rest of the austerity program are scheduled to continue only through March 31, 1990. It has been said that wage–price controls are "a horse that is a lot easier to get on than to get off." Holding back Mexico's inflation even to current levels may become a problem then. If so, the additional inflationary effects of a major devaluation

Chart 12

Changes in Mexican Central Bank Reserves

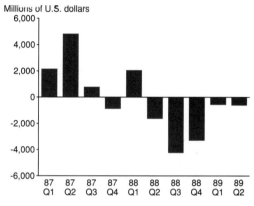

Millions of U.S. dollars

may also be in the cards. And if they are, further capital repatriation problems may develop.

In conclusion, Mexico is showing signs of turning the corner (Table 4). Output is rising. Investment and exports are increasing, and inflation is falling.

But Mexico still has serious problems (Table 5). Mexico's debt problems are not going to be completely solved by the Brady Plan, and capital shortages are already a problem. Investment is not consistent with the rates a developing country may need to compete with its Asian rivals. And, finally, reacceleration of inflation clearly exists.

Table 4
Mexico: The Good News

- Mexico is growing.
- Investment is growing.
- Exports are rising.
- Inflation is falling.

Table 5
Mexico: The Bad News

- Mexico's debt problems are still serious.
- Investment is insufficient.
- Exchange-rate instability is possible.

The Challenges of the International Marketplace: The Far East

Lawrence B. Krause

S aying that business increasingly lives in an interdependent world and must compete in a global marketplace and that there will be further development in this direction in the 1990s has become cliché. The truth of this proposition was proven in October 1989, when the U.S. and other stock exchanges were shaken by increasing interest rates in Europe and Japan and then calmed when the Japanese market corrected itself. In fact, the whole process started because the U.S. dollar was too strong. Clearly, developments in one country and in one market affect all others.

But does that mean that all countries are the same? Obviously not. Countries have some independence. Global economic stimuli are put through a national filter that has its own characteristics because of peculiarities of national history, culture and ideology. There is also room for different national policies.

However, and this is an important point, the amount of space for national independence is limited. Hence, the economic performance of different countries can be quite similar. France performs very much like Germany; Brazil, like Argentina; Taiwan, like Korea; Singapore, like Malaysia; and Canada, like the United States. We can conclude that neighbors matter. An interesting question is, from an economic viewpoint, in which neighborhood was it best for a country to be in recent years? The answer is clearly the Pacific Basin.

The Pacific Basin—the Most Successful Region

For the past 25 years, the fastest-growing countries in the world have been in the Pacific Basin, and this has been particularly true during the 1980s. The contrast between regions has been stark. For most of the decade, Europe stagnated with unemployment rates near 10 percent (although Europe has recovered during the past two years). Latin American countries during the 1980s have seen their economic situation deteriorate so badly as to rival the Great Depression of the 1930s. The situation in Africa deteriorated from what was already a meager existence.

Yet in the Pacific Basin, major economic advances have occurred. For some countries, such as South Korea, the best decade ever was the 1980s. In 1988, of the 14 countries that participate in the Pacific Economic Cooperation Conference (PECC), four had growth rates of 11 percent or above, four grew between 7 percent and 9 percent and five grew between 3 percent and 6 percent; only New Zealand had minimal growth, but it still showed an increase from 1987.

Why has the economic performance of the Pacific Basin been so outstanding? It is certainly not because of external conditions, which were the same as those that affected other countries. Korea had as much external debt in 1982 as Mexico, Argentina and Brazil. Malaysia, Indonesia and Thailand had as severe a terms-of-trade deterioration as Chile and Venezuela. And the Philippines had as much political instability as almost any developing country, short of Lebanon. What, then, can be the explanation?

Clearly, the factors of importance must be internal to these countries. Four or five possibilities come to mind. First, these countries are all committed to economic growth as the primary goal of economic policy. Other goals, such as income distribution and environment, are given lesser status.

Second, savings and investment rates in these countries are unusually high. Singapore is the champion saver, but savings in Korea, Taiwan and Japan are very high by world standards.

Third, governments follow market-conforming economic policies and are outwardly oriented. Most governments try to influence the market, but rather than trying to reverse its judgment, they just try to push it along at a faster pace and correct market deficiencies.

Fourth, people work hard in these countries—a factor frequently overlooked. Finally, there may be a regional factor at work in the sense that there is a general expectation throughout the region that growth will occur, and this becomes in part self-fulfilling.

One of the most striking characteristics of the Pacific Basin is Japan's growing economic strength. Indeed, Japan has been described as an economic superpower and a political pygmy. This dichotomy cannot continue. Therefore, one should expect a much more active and aggressive Japan during the 1990s.

Will Economic Progress Continue?

There are always uncertainties as one attempts to look forward and make economic forecasts. What clouds the picture in the Pacific Basin is politics. Three countries—China, Japan and Korea—have had considerable political disruptions in recent months, and these events cast doubt on the continuation of economic progress. In China's case, the political changes may appear more drastic outside the country than within it. Indeed, knowledgeable observers of China are surprised that others are surprised by what happened there.

In Japan, having three different prime ministers in a matter of weeks is unusual, as is witnessing the Liberal Democratic Party (LDP) losing an election and facing the prospect of yet another electoral defeat. However, political change in Japan seems to have little impact on economics there. Economic growth continues.

In Korea, there seems to be a negative correlation between political stability and economic growth: in 1988, multiple labor disputes arose, yet the economy grew by 12.2 percent, the fastest in the Pacific. Of course, political uncertainty will cause economic distress in time, but in Korea the politics seem to be calming down before that happens. Hence, political uncertainty does not seem to be derailing economic progress.

Regarding the other systemic factors, none seems to be ending, although they could ebb in time. What seems to be happening is that different countries become the growth leaders. Thailand and Malaysia might replace Taiwan and Korea, and Indonesia might replace Thailand. Hence, there is continual stimulus in the region.

The regional identity of the stimulus seems to come from three factors: international trade, direct investment and tourism. Because these are outwardly oriented countries, international trade matters a great deal to them. Hence, it is important to note that on average two-thirds of each country's exports go to other countries within the region (measuring the region by participation in the PECC).

Recently, foreign direct investment (FDI) has been the most important factor in the region's economic growth. The United States has long been a large investor in the region, but now Japanese investors dominate. In addition, Taiwanese and Korean investors are establishing plants elsewhere in the region. This has an important consequence of stimulating multiple economic contacts.

Finally, tourism is literally exploding in Pacific countries. Korea, Australia, Thailand, Singapore and Taiwan are all recording double-digit growth in tourism. Even Japan is enjoying growth in tourism earnings, as well as a huge rise in tourism expenditures. These are the links that are pulling the region closer together.

Consequences for the United States

What does Pacific dynamism mean for the United States? Each of the Pacific Basin countries is going through industrial catch-up, and it is the United States that is being caught. There is no longer a safe market anywhere that does not feel the presence of competitive products from the Pacific.

However, rapid advancement also means growing markets. It is in the Pacific that U.S. exporters will find their customers. Whether we can compete effectively for those markets depends on us. Will we put our fiscal house in order? Will we have lower real interest rates, which would permit the dollar to fall to a more competitive level? Will the savings rate in the United States rise to permit more domestic investment without borrowing from abroad? Will we improve our educational system so that our human resources are more fully developed? If the United States cannot meet the challenge in the Pacific, it will not be able to compete anywhere. The economic future of the United States will be determined in the Pacific. It is a great opportunity for us.

Critical Issues

"If one sincerely wants to restore the health of the financial-services industry, easing the burden of idle nonearning assets would be a constructive step—and should be done at the earliest possible time."
—Jerry L. Jordan

"Public finance programs can do more to share the risks and to leverage the investments of private lending institutions. But banks have to acknowledge this potential and use it."
—Keren Ware

"Exxon's alleged deceptions and irresponsible erosion of vigilance, whatever the merits of the charges, will have serious consequences for all producers who face increased environmental regulation."
—John A. Baden

"Even though oil prices will increase, oil will become less important to the Southwest economy because the region will produce less of it."
—Stephen P.A. Brown

The Role of Financial Institutions in Economic Development

Jerry L. Jordan

I appreciate this opportunity to share with you my thoughts about a topic of mutual interest to us—the financial industry and its impact on economic development. I will argue that the Southwest regional economy, as well as the national economy, will be more prosperous in the decade ahead if certain reforms are implemented to establish a sound and efficient banking system. In turn, an individual bank's performance is tied to the long-term growth and stability of the market area it serves.

Since the mid-1980s, the Southwest economy has been hit by global economic forces that were beyond the control of local leadership. These include falling agricultural prices and the 50-percent decline in oil prices, which decimated the region's energy industry. Moreover, the dependence on federal defense spending of some communities in the region has made them vulnerable to what appears to be a long-term reduction in the nation's military budget. In addition, the continuing restructuring of America's industries, which is necessary to remain competitive in the international arena in the 1990s, suggests that the agenda for the Southwest must also emphasize those issues that affect the development of less-developed countries. Fortunately, there is much to be learned by all of us from the past experience of other regions and countries.

Forces of Economic Development

The factors that are commonly associated with economic development are easy to identify. Although the conditions that tend to inhibit economic growth and progress are also relatively easy to recognize, they often arise from political choices that are not readily reversed.

As an example of the important role that strong financial institutions can play in a region's economic performance, let me refer specifically to the

Southeastern states—the so-called *Golden Triangle*, which includes North Carolina, South Carolina and Georgia. We saw the region rise from below national average economic performance in the 1950s and 1960s to above national performance by the late 1970s. In Arizona, we have seen economic growth at well above the national average during the past decade. And, of course, California and the Pacific Northwest have enjoyed rapid growth.

The experience of the Southeastern region of the country illustrates how strong financial institutions—and the move toward statewide branch banking and interstate banking through a regional compact—helped to create one of the most economically vibrant regions of the country.

The Foreign Experience

The historical contribution of the financial system to the progress of today's western industrialized economies is widely acknowledged. Also, the role of financial institutions and the financial system in economic development has been studied extensively with regard to less-developed economies of the world.

A study released earlier this year by the World Bank regarding financial systems and development was directed at the circumstances in less-developed countries in Latin America, Asia and Africa. However, the analysis applies equally well to regional economic development within the United States.

To quote from the World Bank study, "A financial system provides services that are essential in a modern economy.... Access to a variety of financial instruments enables economic agents to pool, price, and exchange risk. Trade, the efficient use of resources, saving and risk-taking are the cornerstones of a growing economy."[1]

The developments that we have witnessed in the U.S. Southwest in the past decade are not unique. The World Bank study notes, "In recent years financial systems came under further stress when, as a result of the economic shocks of the 1980s, many borrowers were unable to service their loans. In more than 25 developing countries, governments have been forced to assist troubled intermediaries. The restructuring of insolvent intermediaries provides governments with an opportunity to rethink and reshape their financial systems.... Conditions that support the development of a more robust and balanced financial structure will improve the ability of the domestic financial systems to contribute to growth."[2]

The World Bank study stresses the importance of an efficient financial system. It is worth quoting extensively.

> Financial systems provide payment services. They mobilize savings and allocate credit. And they limit, price, pool, and trade the risks resulting from these activities. These diverse services are used in varying combinations by

households, businesses, and governments and are rendered through an array of instruments (currency, checks, credit cards, bonds, and stocks) and institutions (banks, credit unions, insurance companies, pawnbrokers, and stockbrokers). A financial system's contribution to the economy depends upon the quantity and quality of its services and the efficiency with which it provides them.

Financial services make it cheaper and less risky to trade goods and services and to borrow and lend. Without them an economy would be confined to self-sufficiency or barter, which would inhibit the specialization in productions upon which modern economies depend. Separating the timing of consumption from production would be possible only by first storing goods. The size of production units would be limited by the producer's own ability to save. Incomes would be lower, and complex industrial economies would not exist.[3]

The *World Development Report 1989* stresses, *"Finance is the key to investment and hence to growth* [emphasis added]." Providing saved resources to other and more productive uses for them raises the income of saver and borrower alike. Without an efficient financial system, however, lending can be both costly and risky."[4]

Finally, "Competition ensures that transaction costs are held down, that risk is allocated to those most willing to bear it and that investment is undertaken by those with the most promising opportunities."[5] As the World Bank researchers applied these principles to a survey of countries around the world, they came to the conclusion that "The biggest difference between rich and poor is the efficiency with which they have used their resources. The financial system's contribution to growth lies precisely in its ability to increase efficiency."[6]

The reason for this, according to the World Bank, is that "Even though the financial system intermediates only part of the total investable resources, it plays a vital role in allocating savings."[7] That is because "smoothly functioning financial systems lower the cost of transferring resources from savers to borrowers, which raises the rate paid to savers and lowers the cost to borrowers. The ability of borrowers and lenders to compare interest rates across markets improves the allocation of resources."[8]

Many less-developed countries of the world have been in situations similar to those in some regions of the United States recently, especially with respect to the depressed real estate in the Southwest.

Liquidity risk is the risk of being unable to sell financial assets quickly, except at a steep discount. In addition, there is a risk that the default of one or a few large borrowers will endanger the whole financial system. This is called systemic risk. Financial risk can be reduced by improving the availability and the quality of information about borrowers (individuals, enterprises, or financial intermediaries), by improving the design and the enforcement of loan contracts, and by enlarging the range of instruments so as to permit greater diversification of portfolios.[9]

Canadian Financial Stability Through Regional Diversification

Other foreign experience, such as that of regions of Canada—and Canada's banking system in the 1980s relative to that of the United States—is also instructive. Various regions and industries of the Canadian economy experienced the same boom–bust cycles that certain regions and industries of the United States experienced during the past decade. However, Canada did not experience the financial industry crisis that occurred in the United States. In addition to Canada's economy experiencing the same extreme fluctuations that we saw in the United States, Canada also has a federal deposit insurance system very similar to our own. Thus, the Canadian experience provides useful comparisons.

The energy-producing province of Alberta experienced an oil boom in the late 1970s and early 1980s similar to that of the Southwestern region of the United States. Subsequently, Alberta suffered a regional depression much like the U.S. energy-producing regions. Two small banks in Alberta, exploiting the moral-hazard aspect of deposit insurance, took on what were subsequently determined to be "imprudent risks" and ultimately failed when the regional economy contracted.

Other large Canadian banks lending in Alberta also suffered losses, but the losses suffered in the depressed regions were covered by continued profitable operations in other provinces in the country because the seven major Canadian banks are all nationwide branch-banking institutions. This feature of Canadian banking allowed the institutions to achieve a considerable degree of regional and industry diversification in the banks' asset portfolios. As a result, the regionalized boom–bust conditions in Canada did not produce the financial industry disaster that occurred with savings and loan institutions and commercial banks in the Southwestern region of the United States.

The U.S. Southwest Region

First Interstate's experience in the Southwest and Rocky Mountains demonstrates the value of having regionally well-diversified institutions. Geographic diversification enables First Interstate to serve the communities in which our banking offices are located during both very adverse times and the best of times. In some communities, such as Lea County, N.M., our bank was the only one that did not change ownership or suffer takeover or outright closure by regulators.

Although it is certainly not pleasant to suffer several years of continuous losses at any subsidiary, it is possible to do so because of the earning power of other affiliate banks. Because our track record proves that we are not a "fair-weather bank," we hope to have earned goodwill and patronage in local communities as better times return to the region.

U.S. Financial Regulation

The banking industry, along with most other industries in our economy, has experienced a wrenching restructuring process. The process is likely to accelerate in the 1990s as our business becomes less regulated and more competitive. There will be less room for error or bad judgment, and efficient markets will weed out the weak players. Let me comment on what I see happening in the areas of pricing of financial services, products offered, place of business and business charter.

We have already seen in the 1980s almost total deregulation of the pricing of financial services, as ceilings on the interest rates that banks can pay depositors have been removed and usury laws on loans have been virtually eliminated.

Product Regulation. Glass–Steagall restrictions on the products that banks can offer, such as underwriting certain securities, are being eroded. Nonfinancial institutions have entered the financial-services business, and the functional distinctions between banks and thrifts have become hardly discernible as thrifts have gained the power to sell services traditionally offered by banks. There still are, indeed, significant anticompetitive restraints in some product areas, such as insurance and the underwriting of corporate debt and equities. I expect that the pressure of international competition, if not legislative enlightenment, will eliminate these remaining barriers in coming years.

Universal Banking. During the next decade all the major industrialized countries will ultimately permit the emergence of *financial supermarkets*. Financial institutions that offer a full array of financial services are referred to as *universal banks*. They have long been in existence in Europe, and, with the economic integration associated with Europe 1992, we will see many global institutions offering a complete line of commercial banking, investment banking, merchant banking and insurance services.

The United States had universal banking before the 1930s, and Japan's *zaibatsu* groups were dismantled only after World War II. Much of the financial legislation and regulation of the 1930s was a big mistake and is being repealed incrementally. The Glass–Steagall segmentation of the financial industry and Article 65 in Japan are anachronistic holdovers that will disappear in the final decade of this century.

The certainty of the global trend to universal banking derives from international competitive pressures. Technology played a major role in breaking down onerous branching and interest-rate regulations in the United States, and it will play a role in breaking down remaining international barriers. Financial institutions operating from a base in countries with the most liberal rules will have considerable advantage over those operating under rigid regulations.

Canada has returned to a banking structure close to universal banking, as have Britain and France. Australia and New Zealand ended the distinction between commercial banks and investment banks five years ago. As the markets for assets and financial services become increasingly global, supranational financial institutions will emerge. Political boundaries no longer create economic boundaries over a protracted period of time, even for goods, and certainly not for finance.

Place of Business. Penetration of markets within states and on a nationwide basis is being facilitated by a system of regional compacts and by the acquisition of failing banks and thrifts by stronger institutions. In 1991, California will allow interstate acquisition of its banks on a nationwide basis, permitting the large New York banks to enter the state. On a reciprocal basis, California banks will be allowed to acquire banks in New York. Thus, the historic McFadden Act and the 1970 Douglas Amendment of the Bank Holding Company Act are rapidly becoming mere symbols of an earlier era.

Imagine what the financial-services industry would look like today had there never been a McFadden Act and a Glass–Steagall Act. Artificial political boundaries such as state lines and county lines would not serve as barriers to efficient branch networks. There would still be small "boutique" institutions serving only a local market and providing only certain specialized services. There might be nationwide chains that position themselves as the high-volume, low-margin "K-Marts of banking." Others might seek to go upscale and become the "Neiman Marcus of financial services." There would be more franchise arrangements where local investors and managers operate under a licensing arrangement with a large financial network. In other words, there is no one model that would dominate. However, we know that a world without Glass–Steagall and McFadden would be much different from what we have had for the past 50 years, and we also know that is the direction in which we are now headed.

Implications for U.S. Banking

For American banks in the 1990s and beyond, the future will be shaped by fairly dramatic forces that are already at work and that are deemed unstoppable. These include the following:

- *Globalization.* Globalization is the interlinking of financial markets around the world and the inherent inability of any major nation to isolate its capital market from events occurring in other countries. Witness, for example, the worldwide stock market debacle of October 1987 or, more recently, the impact on the dollar of political instability in Japan and China. As technology has propelled us into an around-the-clock global financial market, banks have positioned themselves—with offices in Los Angeles, New York, London and Tokyo—to serve financial needs in the international arena. Because goods are traded globally and portfolios of earning assets are globally diversified, some financial institutions will seek the capability to operate globally. The number to be headquartered in the United States, rather than Europe or Japan, remains to be seen.
- *Foreign Competition.* The rise of foreign banks, especially Japanese, on the world scene has been phenomenal and is likely to continue. Of the top 10 banks in the world, eight are Japanese, one is French and only one is American. On a longer list of the top 50 banks in the world, only four American banks appear—a dramatic shift in the world's financial power structure in just 10 years. As recently as 1980, seven of the top 10 banks were chartered in the United States. The relative ranking of profitability has not shifted as dramatically as total assets, but there is no question that U.S. banks are handling a shrinking share of the financial intermediation in the world and even within the United States.
- *Internal Efficiency.* As restructuring progresses and a more free-market environment evolves in the financial sector, the quest for operational efficiencies, low-cost production and high returns on capital will be the dominant concern of bank management.

Within this context, banks are already positioned to be sound and well-managed economic agents in some regions of the nation but not in others. In several states, much still needs to be done to move the regional economy and its financial institutions in a positive direction for the future. Let me highlight some features of the current situation.

- Only 17 states with limited bank branching laws remain.
- In some states the inherent inefficiency of the restrictions on branching by banks was made obvious by the liberal branching powers granted to thrift institutions in the same state. When statewide branching was first permitted for savings and loan associations (S&Ls), their powers had not yet been expanded to allow them to offer the full range of banking services—powers that were subsequently granted by federal legislation in 1980 and 1982. By not easing restrictions on branching by banks in the face of the liberal treatment of S&Ls, a grossly uncompetitive situation

was allowed to develop.

- The trend across the country in the past 10 years has been marked by several states—Texas, Massachusetts, Michigan, New Hampshire, Tennessee, West Virginia and Ohio—changing to statewide branching. Pennsylvania will join this group in 1990. In addition, in the past five years, four previously unit-banking states—Illinois, Kansas, Missouri and North Dakota—changed to limited branching.
- Of the four remaining states with unit-banking systems, Wyoming, Montana and North Dakota recently passed laws allowing statewide branching through mergers and consolidations—though not de novo—thus leaving Colorado as the only true unit-banking state in the nation. Legislation to liberalize branching laws is a perennial issue in Colorado, and there is better than a 50-percent chance that branching restrictions will be relaxed within the next year. Restrictive intrastate branch-banking legislation will soon be an anomaly in the U.S. financial system. Because branching across state lines will come later, multistate holding-company structures will dominate for years to come.

There are many arguments that support the view that branching systems tend to promote economic growth and stability of regional economies.

- Greater diversification and stability of sources of deposit funds can be achieved in the case of widely dispersed branch networks because various local areas have different demographic, income and industrial characteristics.
- Branching helps to make banks' loan portfolios less vulnerable to wide swings in the level of local economic activity, the level of well-being of the region's residents and the financial performance of businesses in the region.
- Economies of scale can be realized in some bank operations—especially through automation—resulting in lower unit costs and lower prices of bank services to customers.
- Branch-bank networks can provide a higher quality service, enhanced products, a wider range of choices and easier access for customers.
- The higher safety and soundness characteristics of banking systems based on extensive branching contribute significantly to the stability of regional economies. I think most people would agree that fewer Texas banks would have failed in the late 1980s if statewide branching had been permitted.
- These trends and arguments imply that the few remaining holdouts will be persuaded to join the rest of the nation in adopting statewide branching. The benefits of such a change to banking customers and to

the regional economy are eroding the local political resistance to creation of a more competitive financial environment.

Deposit Insurance, Capital and Reserve Requirements

If it is accepted that a strong and competitive financial-services industry contributes to real economic growth, then it would seem that governmental regulations and supervision of financial institutions should be designed to foster stability and strength. However, such is not always the case. During the past decade, the moral-hazard problems associated with the present deposit insurance system, in conjunction with inadequate capitalization of institutions in the thrift industry, created a financial industry nightmare, especially in the Southwestern region of the country.

Deposit Insurance Reform. Recent legislation affecting the thrift industry addresses the capital-standards issue of S&Ls while only mandating a study of the deposit insurance part of the problem. Correcting the flaws in our current federal deposit insurance system is essential to achieving long-term stability of our financial industry, and we should not wait until the next crisis to deal with this very fundamental problem.

Among the reform proposals under discussion, a system similar to Britain's has considerable merit. Within the $100,000 limit—which should be per person, not per account—the first $25,000 would be 100 percent federally insured, and the remaining $75,000 would be coinsured by the Federal Deposit Insurance Corp. (FDIC) and private insurers. Alternatively, the depositor might opt for self-insurance of a portion of the $75,000 and avoid the private insurance premium in favor of a higher interest rate.

Capital Requirements. Banking industry regulators in the United States and 11 other countries have agreed on minimum capitalization standards for banks. The objective of the U.S. bank regulators is to force banking companies to raise additional investment capital in their institutions.

The managerial response on the part of under-capitalized institutions, however, has been to constrain the growth of assets or sell assets whose current market value exceeds book value to record an increase in book capitalization. Such actions are causing an increase in relative concentration in bad assets in some of the weaker institutions. Currently, regulators do not permit *marking-to-market* and counting as net worth the appreciation in market valuation of asset holdings, nor have they in the past required the writing down of assets when market value is less than book value. The current emphasis on book-value accounting measures of financial capital creates an incentive to sell the strong assets and retain weak assets, thereby creating the illusion of greater capitalization than actually exists.

This regulatory emphasis on capital derives from government-supplied deposit insurance and the potential loss to taxpayers associated with guaranteeing depositors against loss. Fixing the problem of deposit insurance would also promote clearer thinking about capital adequacy.

International agreements among central banks and the desire to achieve a "level playing field" among international banking organizations may continue to be used to justify minimum capital standards imposed on depository institutions in the future. There is no justification, however, for imposing those same requirements on holding companies in the financial-services industry. The Basle Accord should be applied only to the banking subsidiaries of the financial institution.

Reserve Requirements. An associated problem is that of the minimum reserve requirements on transactions liabilities imposed by the Federal Reserve on all depository institutions. In effect, this serves as a franchise tax on the right to provide transactions services. The amount of the tax is equal to the foregone income on minimum reserve balances in excess of the level that would be desired for clearing purposes—returns on equity and assets are thus impaired by regulation.

The intent behind minimum reserve balances was supposed to be to provide an adequate cushion in the event of adverse clearing drains and to provide a liquid balance that could be used in the event of a run on deposits at a particular institution. However, because the depository institution is legally required to hold such balances at the Federal Reserve Bank—even when the deposits have already been withdrawn under a lagged accounting system— reserve balances do not provide any liquidity. An especially misguided development was the lagged reserve accounting system that was in place from 1969 until the Depository Institutions Deregulatory and Monetary Control Act (DIDMCA) of 1980 mandated a system of simple, contemporaneous, more uniform and universal reserve requirements.

As experience has amply demonstrated, legal minimum reserve balances are neither necessary nor sufficient for the conduct of a stable monetary policy. Further, they have not provided liquidity in cases of deposit drains at large or small institutions. They have impaired the earnings of U.S. depository institutions, so excessive reserve requirements have contributed to the "safety and soundness" problems of the financial industry.

Because legal minimum reserve balances did not perform as expected, deposit insurance was invented. That development created the *moral-hazard* problem, which made matters worse rather than better. So, now some regulators think that minimum capital standards will solve the problems created by excessive and misguided deposit insurance and reserve requirements. Other regulators think that mandating a higher loan loss reserve will provide the cushion they desire to protect somebody from something.

The combination of mandated idle reserve balances, deposit insurance, minimum capital standards and now mandated loan loss reserve balances has created a highly burdensome set of rules that ensure the continued shrinkage of the relative—and in some cases the absolute—size of U.S.-chartered depository institutions. Yet, the demand for financial services continues to expand, and unencumbered intermediaries would often have a natural comparative advantage providing such services in the absence of excessive regulation. Forcing financial flows to find channels other than through regulated depository institutions does not contribute to the safety and soundness of the entire financial system.

Elsewhere in the world, such reserve requirements are in the process of being reduced or eliminated entirely, and U.S. financial regulators should reevaluate the role that this tax plays. The United Kingdom has a reserve requirement of only 0.05 percent, which is causing other European central banks to lower their reserve requirements because of competitive forces associated with the monetary unification of Europe. In 1988, the Reserve Bank of Australia eliminated reserve requirements altogether. The Bank of Canada is also in the process of eliminating reserve requirements because they are no longer viewed as essential for the conduct of monetary policy. The Swiss National Bank, in recent years, has refrained from enforcing its relatively low reserve requirements.

The Federal Reserve could contribute toward restoration of the financial strength of depository institutions in the United States by announcing a program of reducing the reserve requirement on transactions liabilities from the present 12 percent to the current statutory minimum of 8 percent. Furthermore, legislation should be sought to permit further reductions of reserve requirements to zero, or to a level that does not exceed the amount necessary for clearing purposes.

The argument against lowering reserve requirements on the grounds that such a change would reduce the earnings of the U.S. Treasury and add to the budget deficit should be rejected as a cynical response that places short-term political objectives ahead of the creation of a more sound and efficient financial sector. If one sincerely wants to restore the health of the financial-services industry, easing the burden of idle nonearning assets would be a constructive step—and should be done at the earliest possible time.

Concluding Remarks

My remarks today have been about the crucial role that financial institutions play in promoting economic growth. We want to contribute to the ideas that improve the performance of this region and the nation in the future. I hope you will take my remarks about the importance of improving the quality and competitiveness of financial institutions to be constructive.

U.S. financial institutions are facing enormous challenges now, and their ability to compete effectively in the 1990s can be enhanced by prudent regulatory changes. On the global scene, European financial institutions will be stronger competitors as Europe 1992 becomes a reality. Simultaneously, Japanese banks will be repositioning themselves to maintain their dominance in major segments of the financial-services market.

The evidence of the 1980s clearly supports the removal of restrictions against regional and product diversification, as well as easing of the onerous burden of reserve requirements. The free flow of savings and capital, the appropriate pricing of risk, and a wide range of innovative financial services available to consumers and businesses are crucial to an efficient, sound and stable banking system in the United States.

Notes

[1] World Development Report 1989. *The International Bank for Reconstruction and Development/ The World Bank, Washington, D.C., June 1989, p. 1.*

[2] *See* World Development Report 1989, *p. 1.*

[3] *See* World Development Report 1989, *p. 1.*

[4] *See* World Development Report 1989, *p. 25.*

[5] *See* World Development Report 1989, *p. 25.*

[6] *See* World Development Report 1989, *p. 26.*

[7] *See* World Development Report 1989, *p. 29.*

[8] *See* World Development Report 1989.

[9] *See* World Development Report 1989, *pp. 33–34.*

Technological Innovation in the Southwest

Keren Ware

The proposed title of my prepared remarks was "Technological Innovation and Marketing in the Southwest." I did a little triage on that, so I am going to talk a little about technology and a lot about innovation, and I will not get to marketing at all.

Texas and the Southwest are sitting on billions of dollars of virtually untapped potential wealth. This nation and the states in this region have made a tremendous investment in the infrastructures for technological development here in the Southwest.

Just to get all our numbers in the right ballpark,

- The Texas Medical Center has a budget of more than $2 billion a year.
- The Dallas–Fort Worth Metroplex has snagged just under $1 billion of federal dollars for research and development, with nearly half slated for basic research.
- Federal dollars to Los Alamos and Sandia are around $1.5 billion.

Texas supports not one, but two world-class research university systems and a remarkably strong constellation of other educational institutions that captured $600 million in research dollars last year. Those research dollars support general academic research efforts, as well as targeted projects like the Texas Center for Superconductivity. And those dollars supported the ability of the institutions to help the state attract the Microelectronics and Computer Technology Corporations (MCC), Sematechs and superconducting super colliders. And while Texas has had these flashy successes recently, I know our neighboring states have made similar kinds of investments in their research infrastructure.

Almost every organization I have mentioned, though, is a research and development institution. Research and development falls into a category of activities I like to call *invention*, coming up with new ideas.

I want to talk a little about the difference between invention and innovation. If invention is new ideas, innovation is ideas applied to the market for the first time. For example, when people talk about the loss of U.S. technological competitiveness, they are not talking about *invention*. We are still the world's leading source for revolutionary technological ideas. They are talking about *innovation*—essentially our ability to turn those ideas into money, business ventures and jobs.

The *de rigueur* example everyone uses to show the tenuity of the geographical connection between invention and innovation is, of course, the videocassette recorder, which, as we all know, was invented in California and for which our dollars go to Japan. Long before that, Sony was selling us consumer electronics using its improvements on Western Electric's transistors. Kawasaki developed Unimation's industrial robots further and revolutionized Japanese productivity long before these changes were implemented here. More recently, the Japanese have begun working on applications of the high-temperature superconducting materials that they are confident we will develop—unless they get there first.

So, we are beginning to get over the naive expectation that if we just stay ahead in research and development (R&D), all our work not only will push the frontiers of science but also will naturally lead to new products, enhanced productivity, new business development and more competitive industry. Sure, R&D will do all those things—but where? Baden–Württemberg? Tokyo? Singapore? Texas? This problem is generic to the United States, not Texas or the Southwest. Reaping the benefits of American technological investments is a concern everywhere, probably one you have already heard a lot about.

In the remainder of my time, I will touch on two things closer to home. First, I will tell you about what Texas has done to foster invention and innovation to benefit the state. Second, I will talk about some of the barriers to our success. I apologize upfront for being a bit provincial. When talking about support for technological innovation, I know Texas best, so I will talk about Texas.

But rather than reciting a laundry list of policy initiatives, let me tell you what one start-up company told us recently. DTM Corporation, a small Austin start-up firm that has received national and international attention for its innovative manufacturing prototyping technology, testified before the Texas House of Representatives' Science and Technology Committee on how the firm had been affected by some recent policy initiatives. DTM's technology was developed by a graduate student in the engineering department of the University of Texas at Austin.

The firm told the committee that
- The fledgling company had received critical early-stage assistance from the University of Texas' Center for Technology Development and Transfer;

- Clarifications of state and university intellectual property policies had been essential for the company to have been created;
- The students' and the university's ability to hold equity in the start-up firm had been critical to the venture's success; and
- Seed funding for the work had come from the state's advanced technology program and then from federal research funds.

It is impressive that, except for the federal funds, none of these elements existed before 1987. These and other initiatives Texas has introduced center on improving the research and development infrastructure, enhancing the R&D environment, facilitating technology transfer from the university environment and improving the likelihood of technology commercialization.

The legislature addressed the commercialization issue more directly in 1989, creating the Product Commercialization Fund and putting the Product Development Fund on the November ballot (and it subsequently passed).

So, we are hearing from companies like DTM that we are doing some things right. The state passed initiatives improving the working environment for research. We have the nation's largest competitive research grants program. We have all these magnificent resources—NASA, SSC, MCC, Sematech.

Does this mean that we are poised to launch right into the economic recovery that will be fueled by this investment? Far from it! Instead, I suggest that we are just building up a greater backlog of unfulfilled potential.

What must happen to technology—to invention—for it to become fully exploited as innovation? Obviously, regardless of where technology is developed, it is a business that must latch on to it and decide to run with it. It is not for the university, or the medical center, or NASA, or even a consortium like MCC to refine its research, study the market, manufacture a product and then market and sell it. Some institutions have attempted this process or have created businesses to do that, but in general it is not appropriate to put the burden of technology commercialization—of innovation—on them. Private business bears that responsibility.

In 1989, I see two barriers between us and the successful exploitation by businesses of our inventions and our technology resources in the 1990s:

1. Getting more Southwest businesses to take advantage of the available research resources
2. Obtaining financing for all stages of the innovation process.

I can speak at length about the need for businesses in Texas and the Southwest to take better advantage of our university and federal laboratory resources and about some of the reasons that does not happen more. I will be happy to do so if there is a question about it later. But this is a common problem throughout the United States today.

It is the second barrier that is more particular to the Southwest and more immediately serious. This barrier is financing—financing for the development and expansion of high-technology businesses.

I travel around the state frequently now, and I have listened to what people are saying about their ability to get financing. Because I was scheduled to speak at this conference and finance is not my field, I have asked people around the state for their thoughts on financing. I have talked to venture firms, investment bankers, small businesses, agribusinesses, high-tech companies that have received funding and high-tech companies that might have been.

What I have heard is that start-up companies cannot get early-stage venture capital. We knew that, of course. Early-stage investors like to have a local lead investor, and not enough firms in Texas do that kind of work. Of the estimated $239 million in financings by Texas venture capital firms in 1989, less than $9 million was provided to start-ups of any type—high tech, retail, fast food. No seed investments were reported.

The difference between problems we have always had and what I am hearing about today is that the few Texas venture firms that do finance early-stage ventures are beginning to have a problem bringing in those critical out-of-state partners. It is not that the deals are not good; it is that the out-of-state venture firm looks at the Texas banking situation and says, "Why should we help you finance a start-up venture in Texas? No matter how well this company does on *our* dollar, when it gets ready to expand it will never get the bank financing it needs."

That is the venture story.

The problem is not just for start-up businesses, however. The many, many more small businesses that are up and running, that want to respond to their competitive environment, that want to diversify their product lines or add new capabilities, are telling me the same thing. That wonderful high-profile company I talked about earlier, that got all the international press and testified before the legislature, ultimately was able to get financing—but from out of state.

The more typical companies, less glossy but also more established, are saying, "We can cash-flow the financing we are looking for. We talk to out-of-state banks, and they tell us it is a bankable deal but too small to bother with from out of state. We talk to in-state banks, and they will not touch us with a 10-foot pole."

Others, usually larger companies, tell me they can get financing, but the interest rates are completely out of line with what they understand is available in other parts of the country. In fact, I have been getting similar messages irrespective of the situation—whether it is a high-tech business, an agribusiness trying to diversify, a community wanting to develop value-added manufacturing or food-processing capabilities or a venture capital company.

For purposes of impact, let me summarize what I have heard with the following syllogism, a three-point, logical sequence with frightening implications.

1. We have been told—until we are tired of hearing it—that the future of the Texas economy is diversification. We agree.
2. Diversification *by definition* means, "Doing something you have not done before." Either you have never done it, or you have not done it in this place or with this equipment or for this market.
3. Texas banks are telling us, "If we have not done it before, we are not doing it now. We thought we understood oil and gas and real estate, and we got burned in oil and gas and real estate. It is ridiculous to ask us to do technology deals and agricultural diversification deals and manufacturing deals right now."

Now, I do not want to add to the chorus of people beating on Texas banks. It is bad enough that all the lawyer jokes I used to hear are being recycled as banker jokes. Texas and Southwestern banks have taken a beating and have a lot of crosses to bear right now that have nothing to do with what I, as an economic developer, or Joe Smith, as a business leader, might want to see.

On the other hand, the Southwest region—its technological assets, agricultural resources, value-added manufacturing, any of its economic activities—cannot go anywhere without financing. Great potential is not enough.

Let me review some directions and suggestions that have emerged from my conversations with the technology community. We know that in the 1990s we will continue to see the development of new institutions and new relationships between existing institutions. Public finance programs must do more to share the risks and to leverage the investments of private lending institutions. But banks have to acknowledge this potential and use it.

The Southwest region already has some interesting, nontraditional models for collaboration between a state and a variety of financial institutions: the Oklahoma Investment Board, Louisiana's venture funds and the newly enacted Product Development and Commercialization programs in Texas. The Texas Legislature has indicated a willingness to share the burden of risk for lending in a variety of new situations, such as business incubators, product development and agricultural diversification. We need these, and we need new ways for banks, venture firms, states and the federal government to work together.

We also need to see continued development and support of risk capital networks and other sources of alternative financing to address the seed capital problem. Banks and other financial institutions have traditionally been an important source of informal referrals for risk capital. Studies by the IC^2 Institute at the University of Texas at Austin indicate that billions of dollars can be tapped by the Texas Capital Network and related organizations. So, partnerships and networks are important.

Another issue is expertise. Many banks in our region have had to let many employees go. As unfortunate as this cutback is, when banks rebuild their staffs, they have a perfect opportunity to hire or train people with expertise in Texas' future—technology and diversification—instead of adding more people grounded in Texas' past and present. At the same time, the existing staff must understand that decisions to finance technology businesses will be supported at all levels.

Earlier, I mentioned that invention and innovation are not always tightly coupled geographically. In Silicon Valley, they have been. What distinguishes Silicon Valley is not that all those entrepreneurs, managers, marketers, venture capitalists and bankers were in the same place. Of more importance is that they shared a vision. They shared a vision of what their particular technological specialty—electronics—could do for their community and how it could make them rich.

We have a pretty good jump on that kind of vision here. Many of us are excited about the breakthroughs taking place in this region. On the eve of the year 2000, only 10 years away, we may look back at the spin-offs, the jobs and the dollars created by the super collider and high-temperature superconductivity and by the human genome project and other biomedical breakthroughs, and wonder how all those goodies ended up overseas again.

Or, we may look back and take note of the individuals who broke away from the pack, from expectations, and decided to make the personal and financial investments necessary for the Southwest to enjoy the fruits of its years of technology investment. We will look back and recognize the leaders who opted to participate in the *future* economy of this region and, thus, helped create it.

The Environment and Economic Growth in the Southwest

John A. Baden

I n early 1989, U.S. energy policy was in a state of transition. There was increasing concern about our growing dependence on imported oil, the greenhouse effect and the proposed Clean Air Act amendments. Among the positive developments for the oil and gas industry, America was poised to encourage the use of natural gas as an environmentally superior fuel and to open the Arctic National Wildlife Refuge (ANWR) to oil exploration and development.

However, on March 24, 1989, the picture suddenly changed. The *Exxon Valdez* ran aground on Blight Reef, spilling nearly 250,000 barrels of oil into Prince William Sound. The oil spread over 1,000 square miles, dirtying not only beaches and wildlife but also public opinion. Exxon's disaster has cast an image of the company, and an industry, as uncaring and irresponsible. In the short run, this will benefit domestic producers, especially independents in the Southwest. As a consequence, prospects for opening additional federal lands and waters for exploration were greatly reduced.

Uncertainty surrounds the long-term impact of the oil spill on Alaska's environment and wildlife. The spill also raises important political questions about the future of domestic oil production and energy supplies, as well as the U.S. balance of payments. The Alaskan spill gave environmentalists ammunition for policy changes that may adversely affect the energy industry and the American economy. Exxon's alleged deceptions and irresponsible erosion of vigilance, whatever the merits of the charges, will have serious consequences for all producers who face increased environmental regulation.

Locking Up America's Lands and Waters

More than any other oil spill or blowout in U.S. history, the grounding of the *Exxon Valdez* has immense public policy implications. It again raised important questions about the compatibility of petroleum and the environment. Some of these questions echo from the battle for the trans-Alaska pipeline in the late 1960s and early 1970s. Critics have questioned the safety of tanker transport, the importance the oil industry places on environmental protection and the credibility of the industry to honor its commitments.

The result has been proposed changes in existing regulations dealing with oil transportation, exploration and development, as well as demand for new and stronger public policy to protect the environment. Not only the oil industry but also non-oil companies are being pressured to accept a code of conduct demonstrating their environmental responsibility. Increasingly, environmental politics has become an important feature of the national political scene.

U.S. lawmakers are considering laws to tighten regulation of oil tankers and the oil industry. The legislation is aimed at reforming tanker accident liability requirements, tightening federal regulation of tankers and crews and restricting tanker operations in Prince William Sound and off all coasts other than the Gulf of Mexico.

Several bills require additional personnel; random testing for alcohol; contingency plans for prevention, containment and cleanup of spills; and structural changes in tankers.[1] In addition, a federal court has ruled that companies responsible for oil spills and other pollution must pay the full costs of restoring the environment to its original condition, not just the value of the damaged natural resources.[2]

Perhaps the most significant development from the Exxon disaster is the pressure from environmental groups and their allies in Congress and elsewhere to place a moratorium on onshore and offshore exploration and development in Alaska and the Lower 48. The oil spill is being cited as justification to block drilling.[3]

A yearlong moratorium on oil and gas leasing in Alaska's Bristol Bay has been approved. The moratorium covers 84 million acres of tracts on the Outer Continental Shelf (OCS). The legislation extended moratoriums to Georges Bank off the New England coast, as well as a buffer zone within 50 miles of the Rhode Island, Connecticut, New York, New Jersey, Delaware and Maryland coasts.[4] In addition, oil and gas leasing off the California coast has been delayed for at least one year.[5]

Members of the House and Senate appropriations committees said they will move next year to block leasing off the Northwest coast. The state of Washington has already enacted a six-year moratorium on oil and gas exploration along its coast.[6] In sum, almost all OCS leasing, except in the western Gulf of Mexico, has been halted for at least one year.[7] Ironically, the result will be to push the nation toward increased oil imports via tanker transport and, thus, increased environmental risk.

The Exxon spill has also created indirect costs for the industry in Alaska and elsewhere. In May, Alaska enacted a tax increase on oil from the North Slope. This tax will cost oil companies more than $2 billion over the next 20 years. The bill, which changed the Economic Limit Factor (ELF), had repeatedly been rejected but received a favorable vote in response to constituents' outrage about the Exxon spill. Governor Steve Cowper said, "There's no doubt about the fact that the spill made the political atmosphere different from what it was before." Senator Mike Szymanski said, "The pivotal votes that joined the majority wouldn't have done so without the spill." [8]

The Conservation and Public Finance Spillovers of Environmental Damage: The Case of the Disappearing ELF

Increasing the state's severance tax has been a recurrent issue in the Alaskan Legislature. Proposed changes to modify the ELF were consistently defeated. However, shortly after the *Exxon Valdez* ran aground on March 24, 1989, the Legislature passed a bill raising the severance taxes on two major North Slope fields, Prudhoe Bay and Kuparuk River. The increased tax on production from those fields is retroactive to Jan. 1, 1989. Estimates of the additional costs for these two fields are $2 billion. Many observers blame the spill and resultant strong anti-industry sentiment for the bill's narrow victory. Exxon will suffer less than several of its competitors, for only a small proportion of its oil is from Alaska. The payment of these taxes will go into Alaska's general revenue fund.

Already, the ELF changes threaten billions of dollars in exploration and development on Alaska's North Slope. Citing the increase in taxes, British Petroleum (BP) canceled its marginal Hurl State development project near Prudhoe Bay; ARCO Alaska Inc. dropped its plans to add an additional rig to its Kuparuk River field and canceled its production test program on its West Sak field.[9] Alaska's severance tax changes also threaten the United States' largest oil discovery in recent years, ARCO's Point McIntyre. As ARCO Alaska President Bill Wade said, "If the state increases the cost of doing business, then less business will be done."[10]

Alaska, which is facing a budget deficit, derives 85 percent of its revenues from taxes levied on the oil industry. The changes in ELF, which effectively increase the oil industry's production costs and reduce revenue going to the state, coupled with falling petroleum prices, threaten to worsen the state's financial situation. The adverse effects on the industry's incentives to develop Alaska's oil cause both the state and the industry to suffer.

Alaska's legislators and politicians hope to alleviate the budget deficit by increasing the severance taxes paid by the oil industry. However, as production and revenues from the production tax decline, the state's budgetary strain will worsen. Barring massive new sources of revenue, the state will have to reduce its expenditures. However, it is extraordinarily difficult for politicians to cut programs that constituents view as entitlements.

Legislators and politicians have used oil revenues to fund extraordinary state spending. Alaska leads the nation in per capita state spending. For example, its per capita expenditure is two and one-half times higher than that of Wyoming and almost five times higher than the U.S. average. "Fiscal restraint is an alien concept to Alaskan politicians.... When faced with constituent pressures to increase spending, politicians in Juneau have seen little reason to resist," explain economists Steve Jackstadt and Dwight Lee.

In a paper titled "The Alaskan Oil Spill That Continues Unnoticed," Jackstadt and Lee argued that Alaska's tax revenues are best considered "common property."[11] Because consumers and investors outside the state pay most of those revenues, taxpayers in Alaska have little incentive to resist expansion of government programs. And because no well-defined property rights to government revenues exist, the situation encourages a "wasteful special-interest race for more government spending now, with little thought given to its long-run consequences." In brief, Alaskans have become addicted to large and often wasteful government programs.

The result of this "race" is profligate spending. Several wasteful programs and projects have been started and shelved, costing the state hundreds of millions of dollars. Jackstadt and Lee provided several good examples of these "budgetary black holes." For example, in 1978 the state began a program to promote barley growing. The state spent more than $50 million in loans to farmers, building roads and elevators and purchasing railroad cars for transport. However, most of the projected barley was never grown. At the same time farmers were taking money from the state to grow barley, they were taking money from the federal government not to grow barley.

Faced with a budget deficit, falling oil revenues and declining oil field production, will Alaska's legislators and special interests reduce their demands to maintain current rates of spending? It is not likely. Because of the nature of common property resources—the state budget in this case, users do not face the full costs of their individual actions. It is like two small children sharing an ice-cream soda. The incentive is to drink as much as possible, as soon as possible, because whatever is conserved may be taken by the other.

Because the money appears to come from elsewhere, politicians and special interests have little incentive to spend responsibly. There is no effective mechanism, such as the threat of being voted out of office by out-of-state taxpayers, to constrain their behavior. Given the state's deficit and further-declining revenues, we ask the key political economy questions: Will politicians continue to promise their constituents endless benefits? Will the wealth that Alaska has received from its oil resources continue to be wasted? Unless citizens increase their recognition of the problem and follow with institutional reform, both answers are probably yes.

Inhibiting the Industry

This may be only the beginning. Legislation is being considered in Alaska and elsewhere that would increase not only cleanup costs but also the costs of conducting business in the United States. Pending bills would expand federal authority to penalize companies in the event of oil spills and prohibit oil companies from deducting money spent on cleanups from federal taxes.

A recent development may have even more serious consequences for Exxon's and other non-oil corporation's earnings. Responding to pressure from institutional investors holding more than $1 billion in the company's stock, Exxon recently placed on its board of trustees an environmental scientist, Dr. John H. Steele, senior scientist at the Woodshole Oceanographic Institution.[12] If this new trustee anticipates environmental costs and takes appropriate action, the reform will be a useful one. If, however, the move is only a political play on the part of Exxon and other companies that follow the trend, it could mean billions of dollars with little additional environmental safety.

Environmentalists and investor groups, encouraged by Exxon's acquiescence, have drafted a proposal called the Valdez Principles, designed to "exert economic pressure, possibly including consumer boycotts on companies that fail to address their concerns."[13] The 10 principles are analogous to the Sullivan Principles aimed at discouraging corporate investments in South Africa.

The Valdez Principles require an annual, independent environmental audit of each corporation's worldwide operations and public disclosure of the findings. In addition, companies would be required to disclose any environmental or human risks from production methods or products and any accidents or hazards. Such disclosures may lead to increased litigation against some companies and increased costs of doing business. As outlined, the Valdez Principles are broad and sweeping in their objectives. However, they are also extremely vague. One of the consequences of these new policy proposals is that the future of oil and non-oil firms operating in the United States is even more uncertain.

One reason it is so difficult to predict the flow of policy is that unique events sometimes radically change the political economy surrounding the issue. Thus, the Santa Barbara blowout of 1969 colored a generation's perception of the risks of offshore oil development. As a result, the giant field off Santa Barbara's Coal Oil Point is held hostage to emotional seeds planted a generation ago. The *Valdez* spill, the worst spill in U.S. history, could have even greater effects on the future of America's oil industry and public policy.

Oil in Santa Barbara and Policy in Washington

On Jan. 28, 1969, Union Oil's Platform "A" off Santa Barbara, Calif., blew out, releasing 3 million gallons of oil into the Santa Barbara Channel. The blowout and subsequent environmental damage pitted an apparently careless industry against environmental quality and protection. Union Oil's poor public relations provided prime fodder for radical environmentalists, who equated capitalism with environmental mayhem, boorish insensitivity and a myopic focus on profits at the expense of the environment.

The Santa Barbara spill conditioned an entire generation's response to the prospect of offshore oil and gas development. The message—oil and ecology do not mix—became an article of faith. Despite recent safety advances, the oil and gas industry, and hence consumers, are still paying the price of Union's spill.

When something like the *Valdez* spill occurs, opportunistic politicians are sure to exploit it to win points with environmentalists by exaggerating legitimate concerns regarding offshore oil and gas development. Like Union Oil's 20-year-old errors in Santa Barbara, Exxon's errors will have a lengthy half-life.

Manufacturing the News in Prince William Sound and Santa Barbara

When an oil spill, a blowout or a rupture occurs, conflict between what industry representatives experience and what the media report often follows. This was evident in the Santa Barbara blowout of 1969 and in several other spills, such as those at Torrey Canyon, Platform Charlie, Amoco Cadiz and Ixtoc I. This was also true in the *Valdez* situation where, for example, the media took the opportunity to quote New York Judge Kenneth Rohl's comparison of the spill in Prince William Sound with the destruction at Hiroshima. However overstated Judge Rohl's claim, it captures one's attention.

This lack of understanding between the oil industry and the public has a variety of causes with roots in America's political culture. Especially since the Progressive Era, the public has been highly skeptical of big business in general and the oil industry in particular. This has affected the oil industry's relations with the media. In part, this is true because those who report the news are understandably reluctant to report their errors, no matter how misleading. For example, let us return to 1969 and examine the *Wall Street Journal's* treatment of Union Oil Company.

Most Americans know that after the blowout of Union Oil's Platform "A,"

Fred Hartley, the company's chairman, walked out to the beach, held up a few sodden birds and said, "I'm amazed at the publicity for the loss of a few dead ducks." When asked about the Santa Barbara spill, many people interested in environmental policy recall that incident. They may not remember the specific company, or the name of its crusty chief executive officer, but they remember some insensitive representative of big oil saying, in effect, "It's no big deal. Who cares except a few wacko ecologists?"

However, that is not what Hartley really said. A *New York Times* reporter, not at the scene, said it, and the *Wall Street Journal* reported it as a direct quote. This was not the *National Enquirer, The Star* or even *Time* magazine. It was the *Wall Street Journal*, the paper of record for the business world. By treating the story as it did, the paper established a version of the truth nearly universally accepted by the policy elite. A probable consequence of this chain of events is that nearly all congressmen and senators were conditioned by this erroneous perception of Fred Hartley's alleged insensitivity.

In July 1989, the *Wall Street Journal* published a front-page feature about the culpability of Alaska Pipeline Service Co. (Alyeska) and the Consortium in an article by Charles McCoy titled "Broken Promises: Alyeska Record Shows How Big Oil Neglected Alaskan Environment." Some startling allegations included:

- fabricated environmental records,
- failure to install pollution controls,
- failure to honor a spill contingency plan.

These accusations are being used in lawsuits against Alyeska.

During a briefing of journalists at Prince William Sound in late August 1989, Alyeska claimed to have refuted these allegations in a 14-page rebuttal. Of those in the briefing, only one, the representative of the *Oil and Gas Journal*, had even heard of Alyeska's rejoinder. While the study was not made available to the group, executives' summaries were provided on request.

These discrepancies in interpretation often lead to polarization between the media and the oil industry. The media's sensationalizing and industry's lack of communication skills tend to embitter both groups as they claim and counter-claim. An erosion of credibility follows. As a consequence, the media discounts industry's efforts at remedial actions.

Exxon: A Case of Bad P.R.

Almost 20 years after the Santa Barbara blowout, the *Exxon Valdez* ran aground, causing the most widely covered environmental disaster in U.S. history. What Santa Barbara was to the educated and wealthy of California, the *Valdez* spill is to the ecologically sensitive of the United States. When we look at the *Valdez* disaster in perspective, we will see that Exxon conducted a textbook case of recurrent and protracted public relations screw-ups.

Joseph Hazelwood, captain of the *Valdez*, has been called "the architect of an American tragedy."[14] *Time* portrayed Hazelwood as America's No. 1 environmental enemy. However, several factors besides negligence contributed to the grounding, including personnel cutbacks, fatigue and unclear Coast Guard regulations. A writer for *Time* concluded, "As the ship's captain, Hazelwood bears the ultimate responsibility for the wreck of the *Exxon Valdez*. But his actions were not the only factors that contributed to the disaster."

For example, politicians and industry officials successfully opposed suggestions to study the feasibility of a safer, but far more expensive, trans-Canada pipeline. They promised that tankers carrying North Slope crude would meet new, more stringent standards governing tanker transport. These promises were interpreted to mean that tankers would be equipped with double bottoms and other structural safety features. However, because of a series of political and economic decisions, these standards eroded and increased the environmental risk of oil transport.

In retrospect, the attentive public has declared through polls and letters that these risks are unacceptable. Because the incremental costs of additional protection are not explicit, few consumers will be aware of these costs, and objections will be muted. I do not expect any firm or trade association to mobilize consumers to roll back environmental protection. The issue has become a sacred cow, protected from scrutiny by our increasing affluence.

Exxon and the Alyeska Pipeline Service Co. have come under increased criticism from environmental groups for their response to the spill. Critics have charged that both industry and government are unprepared and lack experience for the consequences of the spill. They claim cleanup efforts are inadequate, badly managed and characterized by considerable confusion. This criticism strengthens opposition to efforts to open the Arctic National Wildlife Refuge and Bristol Bay to oil exploration and development.

Much hysteria has been directed at Exxon. Some customers cut up credit cards sent them to the company; some people called for a boycott of Exxon, and others claimed that the company used the spill to raise gasoline prices. "From the hysteria, one would think that Exxon had deliberately spilled 180,000 barrels of oil off Prince William Sound."[15] What is frequently overlooked is that tankers have safely negotiated those waters since 1977, completing more than 8,000 successful trips.

No matter what Exxon did, critics deemed it too little, too late. Environmentalists, congressmen and others, skeptical about their progress, spent a great deal of time debating the meaning of *treated* and *cleaned*. Exxon's promise to clean the beaches was replaced with a term implying less effort. In addition, Exxon has been accused of obscuring the progress of the cleanup with meaningless numbers.[16]

Whatever Exxon's progress, it appears that the spill could not be cleaned up in the sense that a spill of Wesson Oil on the kitchen floor could be. A lot of oil is captured beneath rocks and in beach sediments, where it is impossible to clean. This oil escaped with each tide and reoiled beaches that had been treated. In those areas, continued treatment reached a point of diminishing effectiveness, and the washing efforts had to be shifted to other areas. Efforts by Exxon to speed the cleanup by using surfactants on beaches and two large incinerators were not allowed. Thus, tons of solid, oily wastes remain for nature to process.

Exxon has spent more than $1 billion on cleanup operations, and the end is not in sight. Members of Congress have urged Interior Secretary Manuel Lujan to sue Exxon to recover the full costs of the damage to wildlife and federal lands caused by the spill. In addition, about 150 lawsuits have been filed against Exxon. The cost to Exxon could run into the tens of billions of dollars.

Politically more important than Exxon's financial and public relations woes, however, are the difficulties that oil interests experienced in their efforts to obtain a hearing for their side of the story. As experience with the Santa Barbara spill suggests, this is hardly a new phenomenon. The oil companies' skills at finding reserves, managing reservoirs, refining products and marketing do not extend into the communications arena.

Not all industry members have handled such misfortune so poorly or been treated so badly by the media. When disasters strike a large corporation, some firms immediately assume responsibility publicly. Many environmental and industry representatives have noted the difference between Exxon's "bungling and evasions" and Ashland Oil's open and forthright response to their spill in the Ohio River. Rather than hedging and dodging responsibility, Ashland Chairman John R. Hall took the first step in cleaning up the spill and taking actions to ensure full recovery of the area.

Valdez: The Best Thing to Happen to the Environmental Movement Since James Watt

It takes the right combination of issues and opportunities to create anger and outrage. Oil spills provide the perfect opportunities for environmental groups. Referring to the Santa Barbara blowout as "an ecological Bay of Pigs," the grounding of the *Exxon Valdez* as "America's Chernobyl" or the Arctic National Wildlife Refuge as "the Yellowstone of the 21st century" works toward that goal. "Images of oil in the pristine, scenic area of Prince William Sound are repeatedly shown as cause for locking up vast new areas of wilderness and thereby making more lands unavailable for multiple use and oil exploration" and for creating anger and outrage to get people involved.[17]

In 1969, residents of Santa Barbara organized into groups. The first was GOO! (Get Oil Out). GOO! took a militant stance against oil exploration and development, calling for a halt to all drilling in the Santa Barbara Channel. At the national level, the Center for Law and Social Policy was created specifically to fight proposed oil-leasing development. In general, environmental organizations benefited from Union Oil's disaster. One member was quoted in *Newsweek* as saying, "That mess did us more good than a million words in Congressional testimony."[18]

At the time, Sierra Club members and others called for a moratorium on offshore drilling in the Santa Barbara Channel and elsewhere. After the *Valdez* accident, environmental groups held a news conference to chastise not only industry's response to the spill but also that of the government. The sentiments expressed at the conference and throughout the press have strengthened opposition to further leasing, exploration and development in Alaska and elsewhere. In fact, these groups are calling for a ban on any further oil exploration and development in Alaska, particularly in the Arctic National Wildlife Refuge (ANWR), Bristol Bay and offshore in the Chukchi Sea. This increases the value of existing reserves in the Southwest much as the Wilderness Act of 1964 increased the value of privately owned timberland. In other words, alternative supplies were locked up.

The Sierra Club Legal Defense Fund and the Trustees for Alaska are suing Exxon and Alyeska on behalf of a coalition of environmental groups. The purpose is to require industry to clean up Prince William Sound and to improve its ability to respond to spills.[19] Robert Young, an official in Exxon's Exploration, Land and Regulatory Affairs Department, has voiced a concern that can be traced back to the Santa Barbara blowout, when he said, "The spill is being used by environmental groups in an increasingly aggressive phase of wilderness politics."[20] The sentiment expressed in this statement and the pending litigation provides evidence of trends within environmental politics that have been developing over the past 20 years.

At the national level, environmental groups have become large, professional organizations and corporations. For example, the Wilderness Society has grown from 37,000 members in 1981 to 295,000 members in 1989. The Sierra Club and the Natural Resources Defense Council have also grown considerably, from 181,773 and 29,600 members in 1980 to 500,000 and 90,000 members, respectively, in 1989. For these three organizations alone, the increase in membership has been well more than 120 percent. This increase is evident in the multimillion dollar budgets of the largest organizations—the Group of Ten—and their cadres of executives composed of lobbyists, litigators and experts.

Gone are the days when the environmental movement was largely a movement of "nature lovers who joined in the National Audubon Society's Christmas bird count, hiked with the Sierra Club or fished with the Izaak Walton League."[21] Increasingly, environmental groups are playing a political game: lobbying, publishing and attracting public attention.

William Proxmire, the former Democratic senator from Wisconsin, called the environmental lobby "the most effective one in Washington."[22] This movement from grass-roots environmentalism reflects the push toward national action in the political arena. This move was encouraged by the Reagan administration's policies toward the environment. In particular, the appointments of James Watt as Secretary of the Interior and Anne Gorsuch–Burford as head of the Environmental Protection Agency (EPA) helped environmental groups' funding and membership campaigns.

Watt's appointment came when most people were becoming more aware of the environment and the consequences of man's careless activities on environmental quality. As the archfiend who would "sell-it-all-before-the-millennium," Watt was the strongest argument for environmental activism.[23]

Watt's apparent lack of concern for the environment was a boon to the environmental organizations, in some instances more than doubling membership. As Lucy Blake, the executive director of the California League of Conservation Voters, said, "You need to create anger and outrage to get people involved."[24] Apparently, she was right. However, after Watt's resignation in 1983, some membership totals began to drop off. In fact, most organizations lost members, some with an annual dropoff rate as much as 30 percent. This means that new members must be recruited just to stay at the same level. Because more environmental organizations are funded through membership dues and contributions, recruiting is very important.[25] Therefore, to sustain their budgets, they must be sensitive to marketing opportunities.

Environmentalists have used the recent accident in Prince William Sound to polarize feelings about oil exploration and development in Alaska and elsewhere in the United States. "Some environmental groups see publicity about the accident and sluggish clean-up efforts as a chance to spur an environmental renaissance."[26] The conflict between environmental groups and the energy industry has fueled one of the most intense debates in the past few years. In the past, environmental groups have focused their efforts primarily on lobbying Congress to expand the EPA's powers and funding. In the fight against oil and gas, they have retained their faith in federal regulation.

At the national level, one of the most outspoken opponents of oil and gas leasing and development in Alaska, particularly in the ANWR, has been the National Audubon Society. The National Wildlife Federation, the nation's largest conservation group, also strongly opposes oil and gas development in Alaska. Together with the Natural Resources Defense Council and the Trustees for Alaska, the National Wildlife Federation published a study of the effects on wildlife and the environment of oil development on Alaska's North Slope. The study accuses the industry of creating an alarming number of environmental problems and of violating environmental laws and regulations. The message to the public is that money is far more important to the oil companies than is environmental quality. This group of environmental organizations conclude that development in sensitive areas of the Arctic is inappropriate.

The Sierra Club has actively lobbied to influence decisions about oil and gas leasing, not only in Santa Barbara but also in Alaska. The club adamantly opposes any development in the ANWR and is currently filing suit with the Trustees for Alaska against Exxon for the *Valdez* spill. Michael McCloskey, Sierra Club president, said the spill "has damaged the credibility of the oil industry in its claim that the prudent development of oil resources in sensitive and delicate environments is possible."[27] Like most other national environmental organizations, the Sierra Club has relied on and strongly advocates increased government regulation to solve environmental problems.

The Wilderness Society has also actively opposed opening the ANWR to oil and gas development. That group cites a U.S. Fish and Wildlife Service report that documents the release of large amounts of drilling fluids and reserve pit wastes into the arctic wetlands, endangering wildlife and the ecosystem.[28] As one group member put it, "the report confirms that oil development has resulted in serious damage to wildlife and habitat on Alaska's North Slope."[29] George Frampton, Jr., president of the Wilderness Society, believes that oil conservation, not development of wildlife preserves, should be the focus of energy policy.

Oil in the Arctic

A recent report by the Trustees for Alaska, the Natural Resources Defense Council and the National Wildlife Federation, titled *Oil in the Arctic: The Environmental Record of Oil Development on Alaska's North Slope,* accuses the oil industry of failure to comply with environmental laws and regulations. The report and the recent oil spill in Prince William Sound support the environmentalists' goal of damaging the public's perception of the oil industry's environmental record in Alaska and elsewhere. As a result, it has become increasingly difficult for even carefully managed oil exploration and development to occur in areas viewed as important for their environmental values.

Well into the future, the United States will depend largely on oil and gas resources, whether imported or domestically produced. Oil and gas do have a potential for environmental damage. However, despite warnings by environmental groups that environmental damage is inherent to oil exploration and development, many experts agree that oil development and environmental quality can and do coexist.

Nearly 6 billion barrels of oil have been produced on the North Slope without significant harm to the environment. While violations of environmental standards have occurred, most have been quite minor.[30] Government statistics indicate that about 45 percent of the oil spilled into the oceans comes from transportation and less than 2 percent comes from offshore production.[31] In fact, the public's perception of environmental damage and pollution results from oil transportation accidents over the past 20 years.

The oil industry has been operating in the Arctic for more than 20 years. Before the *Valdez* disaster, Exxon could point to its North Slope operations as exemplifying oil development without significant harm to wildlife and ecology. While the accident involved oil transportation and not production, the distinction blurred in the public's mind. Nevertheless, 20 years of exploration and production, in which more than 6 billion barrels of oil were delivered without major environmental mishaps, is a reasonable record. More important, it represents 20 years of learning how to develop energy resources in fragile environments. It is this record to which the oil industry points when seeking admission to the ANWR and other environmentally sensitive areas.

The alternative to wrack-and-ruin development is careful, environmentally sensitive exploration and development. If done deliberately, oil and gas can be extracted with little environmental impact. As the National Audubon Society has shown with energy production on its wildlife refuges, oil and ecology do mix—careful exploration, production and transportation can occur while maintaining and even enhancing environmental quality.[32]

Exploration and Production in Environmentally Sensitive Areas

The National Audubon Society's Rainey Preserve in Louisiana shows how well oil and the environment can coexist. Since the mid-1950s, oil companies have run profitable gas wells on the preserve, while maintaining and even enhancing the environment. The society uses fees and royalties from the oil companies to fund purchases of additional land, habitat improvement and environmental education.

The National Audubon Society's Corkscrew Swamp Sanctuary in Florida provides another example. The sanctuary, home to many endangered plants and animals, is also home to carefully managed oil development. Clearly, the National Audubon Society saw exploration and production as being not only compatible with a sound environment if managed correctly, but also in their best financial interest. The Michigan Chapter of the National Audubon Society has had similar success with energy production in a highly sensitive marsh.

Exploration and production activities have also been permitted in other Florida wetlands and in wildlife refuges in Alaska. The oil industry has been allowed to operate in the Big Cypress National Preserve in southern Florida for more than 30 years. Through responsible exploration and production, this development has occurred without harming the ecology or the wildlife of the area. As another example, oil and gas have been produced for more than 25 years in the Swanson River Field, which lies within the Kenai National Wildlife Refuge. This development has also occurred without significant adverse effects on the environment.

The Arctic National Wildlife Refuge

In December 1960, the 8.9 million acre Arctic National Wildlife Range was created for "the purpose of preserving unique wildlife, wilderness, and recreational values...." In 1980, with the passage of the Alaska National Interest Lands Conservation Act (ANILCA), Congress more than doubled the size of the range, increasing it to 19 million acres and redesignating it as the Arctic National Wildlife Refuge (ANWR). In addition, the act created 35 other Alaskan parks, forests and wildlife reserves.

The ANWR lies in the northeast corner of Alaska. The Beaufort Sea borders it on the north, and to the south is the Brooks Ranges. Canning River forms the western boundary, and to the east lies Canada. The refuge is thought to represent the most complete arctic ecosystem and provides habitat to a wide variety of wildlife, including polar bears, Dall sheep, grizzly bears, moose, wolves, foxes, caribou, muskoxen, snow geese, predatory birds, migratory birds and many other species.[33]

Eight million acres of the refuge were designated as wilderness and not subject to resource evaluation; however, 1.5 million acres were identified as potential oil and gas lands. These 1.5 million acres lie in the Coastal Plain, an area 30 miles wide and 100 miles long, which biologists consider the critical area of the refuge because it provides the calving grounds for thousands of the porcupine caribou herd. It is also the area that oil interests and the Department of the Interior are urging Congress to lease for oil and gas exploration and production. While limited geological and geophysical surveys were undertaken in 1984–85, no further development is permitted without explicit congressional approval.[34]

While only limited data exist on the potential of the Coastal Plain, it is considered to be the best prospect for significant oil and gas resources in the United States. The Department of the Interior has identified 26 promising structures and estimated that they offer a 19-percent chance of finding economically recoverable oil. If oil is found, the average recovery is estimated to be 3.2 billion barrels, which would require 10 years to 15 years to explore and develop.

Industry officials, the Department of the Interior and other energy interests feel that opening the ANWR to energy exploration and development is vital to America's energy future. As Prudhoe Bay production declines in the 1990s, the United States is expected to dramatically increase its foreign imports. By the mid-1990s, the Department of Energy estimates that oil imports will be 57 percent of domestic demand; by the year 2000, it will have increased to nearly 60 percent.[35] The industry contends that if production is to be sustained, it has to come from "more intensive development of existing fields, discovered but undeveloped fields or from undiscovered reserves."[36] To that end, 21 congressional hearings were held in 1987 for discussion about the possibility of allowing exploration of the Coastal Plain.[37]

An Environmental Catch-22

Industry's attempt to attain permission to explore the ANWR seemed to be progressing until the *Exxon Valdez* ran aground in Prince William Sound. The result has been an incredible political backlash. The image of the industry as insensitive and uncaring has given environmentalists and others a foundation to believe that oil exploration and production cannot occur in an environmentally sensitive manner. Already, a yearlong moratorium has been placed on oil and gas exploration along the U.S. coast, with the promise of further bans in the future. The debate to open the Coastal Plain will probably continue for years. The result of these developments could be an environmental Catch-22.

The United States already imports approximately 50 percent of the oil it consumes from foreign countries, particularly those in the volatile Middle East. If, as a consequence of the Exxon spill, new production is successfully blocked, the amount of oil that this country imports will increase dramatically, with little reduction in the risks associated with tanker transport.

This will not only increase America's vulnerability to outside events, it will also increase the environmental risk of impetuous action to open federal lands if foreign oil supplies are cut off. This would surely lead to greater environmental destruction. Under these circumstances, if foreign oil is cut off as it was during the embargo of 1973, we are likely to hastily enter the ANWR and other environmentally sensitive areas. Development under these conditions is likely to occur with little regard for the impact on the environment—the very situation that environmentalists and others seek to avoid by blocking new and existing exploration and development.

Energy resources can be developed in an environmentally sensitive manner. This has been shown in Florida, Michigan, Louisiana and elsewhere where oil companies have been given the incentive to do so. America need not sacrifice its environment or energy security in the face of oil shortages. Rather than prohibiting any and all development, we should provide the incentives to the oil industry to explore carefully and inventory our energy resources. Once we determine the amount of energy reserves available, we can devise a plan to prudently develop these resources should, in the event of an emergency, their value override legitimate environmental concern. If conservation and alternative energy sources become commercially viable, environmentally sensitive areas such as the ANWR and Bristol Bay need never be developed. More important, the *Valdez* spill demonstrates the power of environmental interests and the oil industry's lack of skill in the policy arena. Below, I turn to the task of improving the industry's understanding of the political economy of environmental politics.

The Oil Business and the Environment: A Proposal for Exccutive Development

The energy industry is having extremely difficult problems in the environmental policy arena. While it is most apparent in the oil industry, the same problems are occurring in forestry and other areas of natural resources. This has provided wonderful opportunities for environmental groups to mobilize public opinion against business leaders who do not understand the philosophy and ethical background behind these problems.

Below, I propose a program to prepare leaders in the oil business to better understand the environmental policy arena in which they work. My hope is that this will foster economic progress without environmental destruction.

Big Business, the Public Trust and Environmental Stewardship. Environmental policy in North America and Europe increasingly affects business decisions for several reasons. First, events that are perceived as harming the environment, such as the *Exxon Valdez* spill, the Love Canal seepage and the Three Mile Island accident, erode public trust in businesses' responsibility for the environment. As a result, politicians respond to public concern about the environment by promoting regulations of business activities. This is evident in the agriculture, forestry and energy industries in the United States.

Second, environmental catastrophes fuel powerful campaigns for more stringent environmental controls. Unfortunately, these controls often require inefficient means toward sound environmental ends. To an organized environmental group, accidents with implications for environmental quality offer excellent marketing opportunities in the drive for members and contributions. Environmental groups have learned to exploit these problems to promote their political agenda.

Other factors contribute to the growing concern about the environment in North America and Europe. Like gourmet food and foreign travel, environmental appreciation has many of the attributes of a luxury good; it is strongly correlated with increased income and education. As more people become sensitive to environmental values, scientific understanding of man's interdependence with ecological systems also has improved. As a result of increased knowledge, actions previously thought to be environmentally benign are now justifiably restricted because of their adverse second-order consequences. For example, spraying DDT to control the spruce budworm in the Gallatin National Forest in the late 1950s injured the fish, otters and eagles in that system for many years.

This increased awareness and scientific understanding of man's impact on the environment has strong economic implications throughout Europe and North America. Businesses that are perceived as harming the environment and as being politically vulnerable are constrained, and they may be required to mitigate the environmental effects of their actions. Private and governmental organizations increasingly monitor actions expected to adversely affect the environment. They often mobilize in anticipation of, or in response to, environmental disturbances. This is especially obvious in Alaska and the Northwest.

Observers with the background to understand the environmental policy process do not find this spiraling of environmental concern surprising. People in business are often frustrated by environmental politics and often fail to see how economic progress can be reconciled with ecological integrity. This is not surprising because few business people claim to understand the causes and patterns of environmental action. Further, benefits to human welfare are small or absent, and the costs are often far higher than necessary. No program currently exists to provide such understanding.

Businesses must demonstrate environmental concern in their daily decisionmaking. Barring a truly major catastrophe, such as depression or war, these ecological considerations will continue to influence business operations. Yet, businesses will systematically engage in environmentally beneficial behavior that consumes real resources only when doing so serves their interest. To expect otherwise would be naive. The key to responsible reform of environmental policy lies in the recognition that institutional change is required to align the incentives faced by the firm's decisionmakers with the integrity of the ecological system.

People in businesses could benefit greatly—economically, psychologically and in terms of their ecological stewardship—if their leaders better understood how the environmental policy process operates. Unfortunately, no executive business program effectively prepares them to do so. The rationale for, and core elements of, an executive environmental program are presented below.

Rationale for an Environmental Program in Business. Until recently, many business people and academics in business schools seemed to believe that environmentalism was a fad meriting little attention. Business schools have not responded decisively to the long-term presence of environmental concern because the benefits of dealing effectively with these concerns have not been widely recognized. Business school curricula reflect this perception.

We can understand why business academics have avoided this new and vexing area. Environmental matters consistently have two attributes: they are technically complex and highly emotional. Further, most academics in environmental fields distrust business. They believe business will sacrifice the environment in favor of profits, but they often fail to understand how perverse policy incentives foster this outcome. And, among environmental activists, business school academics are usually viewed with suspicion, if not hostility. It is no wonder there is so little communication between fields.

There is an excellent opportunity for a business-and-environment executive or MBA program. It could follow the MBA core in the same way that real estate or advertising does now, or it could be designed as a separate program for executives. Because the topic has not been covered in the traditional business school curriculum, few business school faculty or administrators have the academic background (and few claim an empathic understanding of environmentalism) to design and implement such a program. It often happens that faculty seldom exchange ideas with their colleagues in system ecology (let alone in the philosophically radical deep ecology), and they rarely consort with environmental activists. (Most of those who are comfortable with this area have come from natural resource areas, such as forestry or energy economics and policy analysis.)

Core Elements of a Business and Environment Program. To provide a strong foundation for understanding environmental policy, the program's core includes the following four courses:

• History of Environmental and Natural Resource Policy
• Environmental and Natural Resource Economics
• Environmental Ethics and Philosophy
• The Political Economy of Environmental Policy

We all know that environmentalism did not begin 20 years ago with Earth Day, but few are familiar with the evolution of the movement. To understand the current environmental debate, a historical perspective is very important. The course History of Environmental and Natural Resource Policy reviews the development of American environmental policy since the land acts of the 1800s and the Progressive Era reforms, which created the federal land management agencies, such as the U.S. Forest Service. The legislation following America's great environmental awakening, which began with the publication of Rachel Carson's *Silent Spring* in 1962 and peaked in 1970, lead directly to today's environmental policy battles. A substantial body of literature deals with this topic.

Environmental and Natural Resource Economics is a standard course in departments of economics. Only a small proportion of vice presidents of environmental and governmental affairs in America's major corporations understand this subject. The course applies price theory and welfare economics to the vexing problems inherent to the management of valuable but unowned resources such as air and rivers. The economic logic behind efficient pollution control and the management of publicly owned resources ceases to be a mystery when the analytic leverage of economic theory, especially public choice, law and economics and the Austrian perspective, is applied to these real-world problems. There are at least six standard texts on this topic, and there are a dozen supplemental readers and monographs.

The course Environmental Ethics and Philosophy traces the evolutionary path of contemporary environmental philosophies. The primary goal of this course is to present the shifting conceptions of man's place in nature. This path begins with Rousseau, moves to the American transcendentalists and then to the competing Progressive philosophies of John Muir and Gifford Pinchot. It culminates with today's contending environmental philosophies. The material will show how, after 100 years of experience, the Progressive Era's *scientific management* suffers the fate of centralized planning everywhere. The present-day deep ecologists, bioregionalists and the Greens in Europe and Earth First! in the United States present one alternative for future policy. The New Resource Economics, based on the classical liberalism of Adam Smith, offers another alternative. While there is no standard text on this topic, a vast body of literature covers it in books, such as Samuel Hayes' *Conservation and the Gospel of Efficiency.*

The capstone course of the series is The Political Economy of Environmental Policy. This course examines the outcomes, often unintended, of governmental management of valuable resources. The course examines the problems of concentrated interests and of diffused and hidden economic and environ-mental costs. The potential for creative policy reforms that reconcile increasing demand for ecological integrity with those for economic efficiency and the liberty required for successful free enterprise is emphasized. A growing number of books and monographs address this topic. One example by an environmental professional is Randy O'Toole's *Reforming the Forest Service*. Academics are also writing about this topic, as four of my publications illustrate.

Currently, there is a vacant niche in the academic environment of business. The costs to the energy industry of remaining unprepared are very high. We can also be sure that the corporate foundations will monitor this educational development and look for places to invest. The first school to implement a successful program will perform a great service to the economy and to ecology, and the program will surely be emulated.

Notes

1   *"Alaska Officials Hit Exxon's Fiction,"* Seattle Times, *May 10, 1989.*

2   "Exxon Valdez *Spill Spawns a Batch of Legislation Governing Tankers,"* Oil and Gas Journal, *July 31, 1989.*

3   *"Panel Backs Curbs on Oil Drilling,"* Chicago Tribune, *June 30, 1989, and "Bill Limiting Offshore Drilling Wins Approval of House Panel,"* Boston Globe, *June 30, 1989.*

4   *"Lawmakers Try to Delay Bristol Bay Oil Leases,"* Seattle Post–Intelligencer, *June 30, 1989.*

5   *"Powerful Message Against Oil Leases,"* San Francisco Chronicle, *May 25, 1989, and "Panel Backs Curbs on Oil Drilling,"* Chicago Tribune, *June 30, 1989.*

6   *"Public Participation Needed to Protect State Coastline,"* Seattle Post–Intelligencer, *May 22, 1989.*

7   *"Tanker Spills Spark Fear of Drilling,"* Oil and Gas Journal, *July 10, 1989.*

8   *"Alaska Presses Complaints Against Exxon Oil Spill,"* New York Times, *May 10, 1989.*

9   *"ARCO Blames Backlash for Cancellations,"* Seattle Post–Intelligencer, *June 6, 1989, and "Alaska Tax Increase Shelves West Sak Project,"* Oil and Gas Journal, *June 26, 1989.*

10   *"ARCO Boss Tells Why ELF Needed,"* Fairbanks Daily News–Miner, *March 22, 1989.*

11   *A portion of "The Alaskan Oil Spill That Continues Unnoticed" appeared in the* Wall Street Journal, *Sept. 20, 1989.*

12   *"Exxon Head Seeks Environmentalist to Serve on Board,"* New York Times, *May 12, 1989.*

13   *"Who Will Subscribe to the Valdez Principles?"* New York Times, *Sept. 10, 1989.*

14   Time, *July 24, 1989.*

15   Llewellyn H. Rockwell, *"Exxon Biggest Victim of the Alaska Oil Spill," in* The Free Market, *July 1989.*

16   *"Alaska Cleanup Bigger Every Day,"* Detroit News, *June 26, 1989.*

17   Seattle Times *and* Seattle Post–Intelligencer, *April 23, 1989.*

18   Newsweek, *1969.*

19   Philip Shabecoff, *"As Senate Begins Oil-Spill Inquiry, the Industry Is Roundly Rebuked,"* New York Times, *April 20, 1989.*

20   Seattle Times *and* Seattle Post–Intelligencer, *April 23, 1989.*

[21] *Peter Borrelli, "Environmentalism at a Crossroads,"* The Amicus Journal, *Summer 1987, 24–37.*

[22] *Ibid.*

[23] *Paul Rauber, "A Nasty Split Rocks the Environmental Movement: With Friends Like These…,"* Mother Jones, *November 1986, 35–49.*

[24] *Peter Borrelli, "Environmentalism at a Crossroads,"* The Amicus Journal, *Summer 1987.*

[25] *Paul Rauber, "A Nasty Split Rocks the Environmental Movement: With Friends Like These…,"* Mother Jones, *November 1986, 35–49.*

[26] *Caleb Solomon and Allanna Sullivan, "For the Petroleum Industry, Pouring Oil is in Fact the Cause for Troubled Waters," in* Wall Street Journal, *March 31, 1989.*

[27] *Eliot Marshall, "Valdez: The Predicted Oil Spill,"* Science, *April 7, 1989, 20.*

[28] Wilderness, *Spring 1988.*

[29] *Philip Shabecoff, "Alaska Oilfield Report Cites Unexpected Harm to Wildlife,"* New York Times, *May 11, 1988.*

[30] Oil and Gas Journal, *Feb. 1, 1988.*

[31] Wall Street Journal, *March 31, 1989.*

[32] *John Baden and Richard Stroup, "Saving the Wilderness: A Radical Proposal,"* Reason, *July 1981, 28–36.*

[33] *See James R. Udall, "Polar Opposites,"* Sierra, *September/October 1987, 41–48; Tom Kizzia, "Confrontation in the North,"* Defenders, *September/October 1987, 10–33; Mary Ann Gwinn, "The Last Refuge,"* Outdoor America, *Winter 1987, 6–11; and Donald D. Jackson, "The Floor of Creation,"* Wilderness, *Fall 1986, 12–20.*

[34] *Arctic Slope Consulting Engineers.*

[35] *Charles J. DiBona, "…We Need to Tap Wildlife Refuge,"* Chicago Tribune, *April 12, 1989.*

[36] *ARCO Alaska, On Top of ANWR, March 1989.*

[37] *Patrick Crow and Bob Williams, "Prudhoe Bay 'Pollution' Cited as Reason to Block ANWR Access,"* Oil and Gas Journal, *Feb. 1, 1988, 14–17.*

Energy in the Future of the Southwest

Stephen P.A. Brown[1]

M ost of you are probably wondering why somebody would talk about the future of energy in the Southwest. You may have concluded that there is no future for energy in the Southwest.

Certainly, since 1981 energy extraction has become less important to the region. But by the year 2000, energy will be more important than it is now. Energy will not be as important as it was in 1981, but it will be more important than it is now.

In 1981, energy extraction accounted for about 25 percent of the combined output in four Southwestern states: Louisiana, New Mexico, Oklahoma and Texas. Today, energy extraction contributes less than 10 percent of these states' combined output. But by the year 2000, the figure could be nearly 15 percent.[2]

What has happened to the energy market since 1981? Oil and natural gas prices have declined; the production of oil and gas in the Southwest has declined; other sectors of the Southwest economy have grown. Consequently, energy has become a smaller factor in the region's economy.

But in the next decade, oil and natural gas prices should rise. Oil production will continue to decline in the Southwest, but natural gas production will increase. And even if other sectors grow faster in the Southwest than in the nation at large, energy is going to become a more important factor in the Southwest economy than it is now.

The Outlook for Oil Prices

One can find a wide range of oil price forecasts. The Energy Modeling Forum 11 (EMF 11), organized by Stanford University, represents a consensus of informed opinion. The EMF 11 group consists of energy analysts from the United States and abroad who are studying the world oil market. In their September 1989 meeting, this group of analysts reached a consensus that by the year 2000, oil prices will not be any lower than $15 per barrel nor will they be any higher than $35 per barrel.[3] With oil prices currently about $20 per barrel, there is room for both lower oil prices and higher oil prices within the forecast.[4]

The range of these forecasts is only partially instructive. More instructive are the reasons for the range. The range is very dependent on varied beliefs about the factors that brought energy conservation over the past decade. The analysts who forecast low oil prices over the coming decade generally believe that prices had nothing to do with energy conservation over the past decade. They believe that energy conservation resulted from changes in government policy or magical transformations in the public's desire to use energy.

Other analysts are a little more sophisticated. They think high energy prices did cause conservation. But they think that all of the techniques adopted to conserve energy will not be reversed just because energy prices are lower.

In work that Keith R. Phillips and I did earlier this year, we examined those very issues. We investigated the existence of nonprice conservation and whether consumption responds differently to rising or falling oil prices. We rejected both of those theories statistically. We found instead that oil consumption is very unresponsive to its price in very short periods of time, but it is fairly responsive to its price over long periods of time, such as a decade.[5]

We also found that current oil prices are much too low to be sustained. At current prices, world oil consumption will increase sharply. By the mid-1990s, $25 per barrel could prove to be too low. To sustain a price that low could require too much oil to be pumped out of the ground. By the year 2000, oil prices of $30 per barrel to $35 per barrel could prove to be about right. That would be about 60 percent to 70 percent of the 1981 peak of about $50 per barrel. Our analysis here depends on a price forecast we developed earlier this year.[6]

A word of caution: While OPEC has excess capacity, oil prices could rise and fall sharply. Volatility should not be confused with long-term trends in oil prices.

Oil Production in the Southwest

Although oil prices will rise over the coming decade, oil production can be expected to decline in the Southwest. The Southwest is gradually running out of oil that can be produced profitably. The Southwest has mature fields. Its production actually peaked in the 1970s. In 1981, when oil was at its peak price, oil production in the Southwest was actually at a 20-year low. The decline is also evident in the rig count.[7] The U.S. rig count is much lower now than the last time oil was $20 per barrel. Although recent gains in the rig count are encouraging, the percentage gains in the U.S. rig count are much smaller than the gains in the rest of the world. Furthermore, natural gas accounted for most of the gains in the U.S. rig count over the past year.

To reiterate, even though oil prices will increase, oil will become less important to the Southwest economy because the region will produce less of it.

Natural Gas in the Southwest

On the other hand, natural gas should become more important to the Southwest in the next decade. The Southwest has substantial natural gas resources. A recent estimate by the U.S. Geological Survey indicates that the United States has about a 34-year supply of natural gas at current production and use rates. More than half of those resources are in the Southwest. That contrasts with about a 26-year supply of oil, of which less than 40 percent is in the Southwest.[8]

Furthermore, environmental concerns suggest strong growth in the demand for natural gas. Gas is a much cleaner fuel than either oil or coal. Gas is about 50 percent cleaner than coal and about 30 percent cleaner than oil. As a result, increasingly stringent environmental regulation or market incentives to reduce environmental problems will encourage industry to switch from coal and oil to natural gas.

A third factor could prove even more important. Natural gas prices have been deregulated at the wellhead, which gives the natural gas producer an incentive to produce more natural gas.

Natural gas prices could more than double by the year 2000. The current wellhead price (of about $1.70 per thousand cubic feet) implies a burner tip price that is below parity with the price of oil. Over the next five years, a realignment of energy prices will bring natural gas prices into parity with oil prices. A natural gas price of $4 per thousand cubic feet roughly corresponds to about $30 per barrel, suggesting much higher natural gas prices over the coming decade.

Concluding Remarks

Over the next decade, we are likely to see higher oil and gas prices. At the same time, we should see declining oil production and increasing natural gas production in the Southwest. That should add up to faster growth for the energy sector than for the rest of the Southwest economy—even though the Southwest economy is likely to grow faster than the national economy.[9] In short, the Southwest economy will become more dependent on energy than it is today, but less dependent than it was in the late 1970s and early 1980s.

Notes

1   *This speech was cowritten by Stephen P.A. Brown and Keith R. Phillips.*

2   *See Keith R. Phillips, "Energy and the Southwest Economy,"* The Southwest Economy, *Federal Reserve Bank of Dallas, November 1989.*

3   *These prices and all subsequent prices are in 1988 dollars.*

4   *See Hillard Huntington, ed., "Model Comparison Figures," Energy Modeling Forum 11, Stanford University, presented at Working Group Meeting #2, John F. Kennedy School of Government, Harvard University, September 1989. At the September 1989 meeting of EMF 11, price forecasts for the year 2000 were evenly distributed throughout a range from $15 per barrel to $35 per barrel. By the March 1990 meeting of EMF 11, several analysts revised their oil price forecasts upward in the range.*
    See Hillard Huntington, ed., "Model Comparison Figures," Energy Modeling Forum 11, Working Group Meeting #3, Stanford University, March 1990.

5   *See Stephen P.A. Brown and Keith R. Phillips, "An Econometric Analysis of U.S. Oil Demand," Research Paper no. 8901, Federal Reserve Bank of Dallas, January 1989 (revised April 1989).*

6   *See Stephen P. A. Brown and Keith R. Phillips, "Oil Demand and Prices in the 1990s," Federal Reserve Bank of Dallas* Economic Review, *January 1989.*

7   *Rigs are equipment used in exploring or developing oil fields.*

8   *These estimates include reserves and inferred and indicated economically recoverable resources in place. See "Estimates of Undiscovered Conventional Oil and Gas Resources in the United States—A Part of the Nation's Energy Endowment," U.S. Department of the Interior, U.S. Geological Survey, Minerals Management Service.*

9   *For a long-term outlook for the Southwest economy, see Stephen P. A. Brown and Lea Anderson, "The Future of the Southwest Economy,"* The Southwest Economy, *Federal Reserve Bank of Dallas, November 1988.*

The Southwest Economy: The Next Year and the Next Decade

"Although considerable research talent has been expended to answer the question of whether jobs draw people or people create jobs, the Arizona experience during the past three decades seems consistent with a simultaneous approach—people come to the state looking for jobs and in the process create a demand for goods and services, which creates employment opportunities."
—Lee R. McPheters

"A poorly funded higher education system will be a major deterrent in attracting the futuristic industries of the 1990s to Louisiana."
—Loren C. Scott

"We will have to stop selling our natural resources from out of the ground and sell another type of our natural resources—that is, our mountains, our ski industry and our quality of life."
—M. Brian McDonald

"However different the 1990s will be, surely the 1980s will be distinguished by future generations as the 'decade of debt.'"
—Larkin Warner

"All the major cities in Texas are a bargain, inducing firm relocation and expansion and attracting labor."
—Barton A. Smith

Arizona's Economic Outlook

Lee R. McPheters

B etween 1977 and 1987, Arizona led the nation in the growth of personal income and employment and was second only to Nevada in the rate of population growth (Chart 1). Job creation during this period exceeded one-half million, and population grew by 40 percent. Since the mid-1980s, however, economic growth in Arizona slowed substantially. During the first half of 1989, when national wage and salary nonagricultural employment grew 3.1 percent over the previous year, Arizona's corresponding figure was a meager 1.3 percent, which ranked 41st among the 50 states and well behind many of Arizona's neighbors (Chart 2).

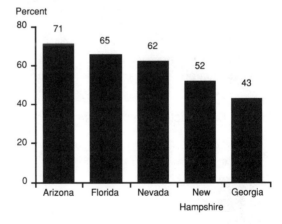

Chart 1
Top Five States:
Employment Growth, 1977–87

In the mid-1980s, several events converged to slow Arizona's vigorous economic expansion. A change in tax laws took much of the steam out of the construction industry, but overbuilding nevertheless was widespread in commercial and multifamily markets. Slowing defense spending undercut the Arizona aerospace industry, while continued pressures from international competitors restricted employment growth in semiconductors. Emerging problems in the savings and loan sector, the construction downturn and defense reductions contributed to the loss of 20,000 jobs in manufacturing, construction and finance between the summers of 1987 and 1989.

At the same time, population flows into the state diminished. From a high of 90,000 in 1985, net migration fell to 36,000 in 1988, the lowest level since the

recession of 1982. Population inflows dipped as job
opportunities declined in
Arizona relative to the resurgent Midwest. Those who
lost jobs in Arizona moved
to other states, such as Nevada or California. (Recent
data from the California
Department of Finance show
that Arizona lost population
to California during fiscal
1988, reversing traditional
interstate population flows.)
One benefit of outmigration,
however, is that it has pre-
vented Arizona's unemploy-

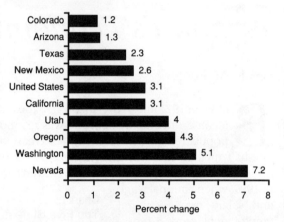

Chart 2
Western Job Creation
(First half of 1989)

ment rate from rising. In mid-1989, the unemployment rate was 5.2 percent,
more than 1 full percentage point below the 6.5-percent level of 1985, when job
creation exceeded 8 percent.

The Arizona Economy in 1989

Construction is one of the key industries in growth-oriented Arizona.
Fluctuations in construction employment have traditionally had a significant impact on Arizona, leading the
general economy through-
out all phases of the business
cycle. After expanding at a
double-digit pace in the post-
recession period, the construction employment
growth rate slowed sharply
in 1986, and jobs were lost in
1987, 1988 and 1989 (Chart
3).

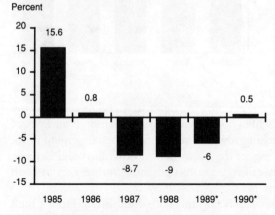

Chart 3
Arizona Construction Employment Change
Percent

* Forecast

During the first half of
1989, residential housing
permits fell by one-third. The

greatest decrease came in the multifamily sector, where permits were down more than two-thirds from the previous year, falling from 5,400 to 1,700. Single-family permits fell by about 20 percent, from 12,500 to 10,000. Analysts' opinions arc divided as to whether multifamily permits will reach 3,000 during 1989. As recently as 1985, nearly 40,000 units were permitted in the state.

Now, more than 38,000 apartments are vacant in the metropolitan Phoenix area, and experts place the vacancy rate between 12 percent and 15 percent (Chart 4). Office vacancy rates continue to hover in the mid-20s. While multifamily building has slowed, the office situation is compounded by the presence of some 5 million square feet of space due for completion in the metropolitan Phoenix area in the next two years.

In addition to excessive inventories of multifamily, commercial and retail space, the state has experienced a steady decline in prices for parcels of raw land. During the expansion that began with recovery from the recession of 1982, land prices rose dramatically, fueled by a process known locally as *flipping*. Some parcels changed hands several times within a few weeks or even days, with each sale yielding a significant profit for the previous owner. Many of these sales were financed entirely by local financial institutions, confident of the character of the buyer and optimistic about the continued health of the land boom. In many deals, the amount financed included sufficient funds for principal payments and interest for two years to three years, until the parcel could again be sold after appreciation. The vast inventories of overpriced land and, less important, office buildings caused the collapse of several savings and loan institutions and are responsible for large losses recorded by most of the state's banks. Six of the state's 12 thrifts are under government control or are insolvent, with foreclosed property of nearly $2 billion and past-due loans of $1.6 billion.

With the exception of the large Valley National Bank in Phoenix, most major Arizona banks are held by out-of-state owners, such as Citibank, Chase, First Inter-

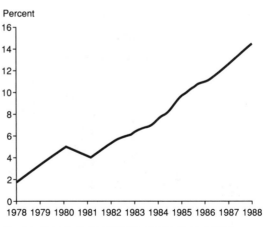

Chart 4

Multifamily Vacancy Rates (1978:4–1988)

Percent

Source: Phoenix Metropolitan Housing Study Committee

state and Security Pacific, whose ability to withstand losses has (so far) lent stability to the state's banking system. Nevertheless, there have been significant job losses in financial institutions. Through August 1989, the state lost more than 2,000 jobs in the finance–insurance–real estate sector, the most such jobs lost by any state during this time, except Louisiana.

Manufacturing has not been a source of strength for the Arizona economy in recent years. Despite the greatest concentration of high-technology employment in the country, Arizona manufacturing has not ballooned in response to the falling dollar. (High-tech accounts for about one-half of manufacturing employment.) After rising by more than 5 percent in 1985, manufacturing job gains have been less than 2 percent in each succeeding year. Through August 1989, manufacturing jobs did not increase at all in the state.

Perhaps the brightest component of the Arizona economy is tourism, buoyed by continuing strength elsewhere in the nation and growing numbers of international travelers. Air arrivals at Phoenix Sky Harbor International Airport continue to set records each year and reached nearly 16 million in 1988.

Between 1985 and 1989, the number of hotel rooms in the metropolitan Phoenix area grew by nearly 10,000, an increase of more than 10 percent (Chart 5). Occupancy rates dipped as room inventory came on line, but then began to rise. Occupancy for 1989 is projected at slightly better than 60 percent. However, Arizona resort and hotel managers have practiced substantial discounting to appeal to convention planners.

Chart 5
Metropolitan Phoenix Lodging
(Rooms: 1985–89)

Rooms

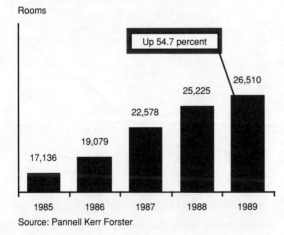

Source: Pannell Kerr Forster

In percentage terms, the fastest-growing sector of the state economy is mining, driven by the copper industry. The growth rate for 1989 is expected to exceed 5 percent. However, there is no copper mining employment in Phoenix, the state's major metropolitan area. In addition, total mining employment is only about 12,000, one-half the size of the mining labor force before technological change and cost-cutting measures reduced employment.

The outlook for 1989 is for a year similar in many respects to 1988. Total nonagricultural wage and salary employment growth is expected to be about 2 percent or less, not far off the 1988 pace of 1.8-percent growth. It is important, however, to avoid describing the Arizona economy in any situation other than *slow growth*. The state is not in recession, as employment continues to grow. Further, population is growing as well, at a pace about double the national average, due to continued positive net migration. Population growth for 1989 is expected to be 2.2 percent, an increase of nearly 75,000 on a 1988 base of 3.5 million.

Arizona's Outlook for 1990

Arizona's outlook for 1990 is based on the assumption of a soft landing for the national economy, accompanied by gradual reductions in interest rates. Lower rates would bolster the single-family housing market and allow construction employment to stabilize after three consecutive years of decline.

The national assumptions underlying the Arizona economic forecast are set out in Table 1. Gross national product (GNP) in 1990 is projected to grow by 2 percent in inflation-adjusted dollars. This increase is only slightly higher than the consensus of 1.8-percent growth recorded by Robert J. Eggert in a poll of 50 economists, as reported in the October 1989 issue of Eggert's monthly newsletter, *Blue Chip Economic Indicators*.

The national assumptions call for a slightly higher unemployment rate of 5.7 percent in 1990 and a 4.7-percent increase in consumer prices. Interest rates are projected to be only moderately lower in 1990.

Most Arizona analysts see 1990 as a year of modest improvement compared to 1989, which they view as the bottom of a period of significant slowing in growth. Real Arizona gross state product should once again increase more rapidly than GNP, after three years of growth below the national rate (Table 2).

Payroll employment is expected to grow by about 2.5 percent in 1990, showing somewhat more vigor than in the past two years but still weaker than the 3.6-percent growth in 1987 and only about one-half the average growth rate since 1970. During the year, about 35,000 new jobs will be added to the economy.

A key component of the forecast is continued population increases at a rate above 2 percent per year. As job creation slows nationally and in neighboring states, net migration is expected to improve slightly. This, combined with natural increases, will cause population to rise by some 86,000 in 1990 for a 2.4-percent rate of increase.

Lower interest rates and a steady influx of people will end the slump in the residential housing market. Activity in the single-family market will rise by 7 percent, to nearly 20,000 units per year in 1990. The multifamily market, still plagued by substantial inventory, will increase by about 3 percent, to approximately 6,400 units permitted.

The inflow of population also dictates those employment sectors that are likely to grow most rapidly (Table 3). The people-serving sectors of both government and services are projected to grow by more than 3 percent in 1990. The slowest growth will be recorded in the struggling financial sector, where the

Table 1
1989 and 1990 Economic Forecasts: United States

	1985	1986	1987	1988	1989*	1990*
Gross National Product Billions of						
1982 dollars	3,618.7	3,721.7	3,847.0	3,996.0	4,091.0	4,173.0
Percent change	3.4	2.8	3.4	3.9	2.4	2.0
Industrial Production						
Percent change	1.9	1.1	3.8	5.7	3.0	1.5
Net Exports						
Billions of 1982 dollars	−104.3	−137.5	−128.9	−100.2	−91.2	−70.5
Housing Starts						
Number in millions	1.74	1.81	1.62	1.49	1.46	1.5
Percent change	1.7	4.0	−10.5	−8.0	−2.0	2.7
Unemployment Rate						
Percent	7.2	7.0	6.2	5.5	5.4	5.7
Consumer Price Index						
Percent change	3.6	1.9	3.6	4.1	4.6	4.7
Three-Month Treasury Bill Rate						
Percent	7.5	6.0	5.8	6.7	7.9	7.4
Aaa Corporate Bond Rate						
Percent	11.4	9.0	9.4	9.7	9.0	8.8

* Numbers for 1989 and 1990 are forecasts.

Source: Economic Outlook Center, College of Business, Arizona State University

Table 2
1989 and 1990 Economic Forecasts: Arizona

	1985	1986	1987	1988	1989*	1990*
Gross State Product						
Millions of						
current dollars	43,505	45,923	46,905	47,795	48,846	50,360
Percent change	8.0	5.6	2.1	1.9	2.2	3.1
Personal Income						
Millions of						
current dollars	40,963	44,766	48,699	52,233	55,785	59,802
Percent change	11.3	9.3	8.8	7.3	6.8	7.2
Retail Sales						
Millions of						
current dollars	16,169	17,187	18,001	18,855	19,892	21,006
Percent change	9.7	6.3	4.7	4.7	5.5	5.6
Unemployment Rate						
Percent	6.5	6.9	6.3	6.3	6.4	6.2
Wage and Salary Employment						
Number in thousands	1,278.6	1,337.8	1,385.8	1,410.6	1,435.2	1,470.9
Percent change	8.2	4.6	3.6	1.8	1.7	2.5
Population						
Number in thousands	3,205	3,330	3,430	3,507	3,584	3,670
Percent change	4.0	3.9	3.0	2.2	2.2	2.4
Single-Family Units Permitted						
Number	33,271	34,079	27,360	22,791	18,689	19,997
Percent change	7.8	2.4	−19.7	−16.7	−18.0	7.0
Multifamily Units Permitted**						
Number	37,312	27,008	12,038	8,853	6,197	6,383
Percent change	−22.0	−27.6	−55.4	−26.5	−30.0	3.0

* Numbers for 1989 and 1990 are estimates.
** Apartment complexes of three or more units.

Source: Economic Outlook Center, College of Business, Arizona State University

Table 3
Arizona Employment Forecasts for 1989–90 (thousands)

	1985	1986	1987	1988	1989	1990
Manufacturing	181.6	184.6	187.4	189.9	192.0	195.3
Percent change	5.1	1.6	1.5	1.3	1.1	1.7
Mining	11.9	11.0	11.4	12.0	12.7	13.1
Percent change	−9.2	−7.8	3.5	5.3	5.5	3.2
Construction	112.1	113.1	103.2	93.9	88.3	88.7
Percent change	15.6	.8	−8.7	−9.0	−6.0	.5
TCPU*	62.9	66.0	71.7	72.7	73.9	75.2
Percent change	5.2	4.8	8.7	1.4	1.6	1.8
Trade	311.4	326.3	340.3	347.5	359.7	368.7
Percent change	8.7	4.8	4.3	2.1	3.5	2.5
FIRE**	81.0	88.9	94.5	93.3	90.4	90.7
Percent change	12.3	9.8	6.3	−1.3	−3.1	0.3
Services	299.9	323.8	345.3	361.2	370.2	383.9
Percent change	9.7	8.0	6.6	4.6	2.5	3.7
Government	218.1	225.0	232.0	240.3	248.1	255.5
Percent change	5.1	3.2	3.1	3.6	3.2	3.0
Total Wage and Salary Employment	1,278.6	1,337.8	1,385.8	1,410.6	1,434.6	1,469.0
Percent change	8.2	4.6	3.6	1.8	1.7	2.4
Total Employment	1,381.0	1,463.0	1,511.0	1,550.0	1,588.8	1,644.4
Percent change	1.5	5.9	3.3	2.6	2.5	3.5
Total Unemployment	96.0	109.0	101.0	104.0	109.9	113.5
Percent change	35.2	13.5	−7.3	3.0	5.7	3.3

(continued)

Table 3—*continued*
Arizona Employment Forecasts for 1989–90 (thousands)

	1985	1986	1987	1988	1989	1990
Labor Force	1,477.0	1,572.0	1,612.0	1,654.0	1,698.7	1,758.2
Percent change	3.1	6.4	2.5	2.6	2.7	3.5
Unemployment Rate						
Percent change	6.5	6.9	6.3	6.3	6.8	6.5

 * Transportation, Communications and Public Utilities
** Finance, Insurance and Real Estate

Source: Economic Outlook Center, College of Business, Arizona State University

growth rate is expected to be 0.3 percent. Manufacturing and utilities will grow by just less than 2 percent, while finance and construction will grow by less than 1 percent.

The retail sector will show very little real growth. Per capita inflation-adjusted sales will not increase, and a decline is quite possible. Retail sales in Arizona have not shown significant real per capita growth since the mid-1980s. Despite this, several major retail grocery and other chains have moved into the state or have plans to do so. In short, the retail environment will continue to be extremely competitive in 1990.

The outlook for Maricopa County (metropolitan Phoenix) parallels the Arizona forecast. About two out of three Arizona jobs are located in metropolitan Phoenix. During 1990, employment in the Phoenix area will grow by 2.4 percent (Table 4). Population will increase by 54,000, about two-thirds of the state total. Net migration is expected to total 26,000 for the year.

The Arizona Index of Leading Economic Indicators gives no signal of either recession or an upturn in state economic activity (Chart 6). The index is a reliable indicator of the strength of economic activity six to nine months into the future. The index soared during the recovery period after the recession of 1982, then it reached an inflection point in 1985. In 1986, the index flattened, indicating a period of sluggish growth. Through October 1989, the index has failed to give the standard recession signal of three months of decline, but it suggests little more than a continuation of the same unspectacular performance recorded for the past two or three years.

Table 4
1989 and 1990 Economic Forecasts: Maricopa County

	1985	1986	1987	1988	1989	1990
Consumer Price Index						
Percent Change	5.0	1.4	4.1	4.1	5.0	5.1
Retail Sales						
Millions of						
current dollars	18,829	11,342	11,743	12,223	12,895	13,617
Percent change	11.2	4.7	3.5	4.1	5.5	5.6
Unemployment Rate						
Percent	5.1	5.6	5.2	5.1	5.2	5.0
Wage and Salary Employment						
Number in thousands	842.4	882.6	913.8	931.3	948.1	970.9
Percent change	9.1	4.8	3.5	2.0	1.8	2.4
Population						
Number in thousands	1,826	1,910	1,976	2,021	2,066	2,120
Percent change	5.6	4.6	3.4	2.3	2.2	2.6
Single-Family Units Permitted						
Number	23,143	23,851	18,012	14,734	11,787	12,589
Percent change	11.4	3.1	−24.5	−18.2	−20.0	6.8
Multifamily Units Permitted*						
Number	27,271	18,311	9,106	6,160	4,004	4,104
Percent change	-25.9	−32.9	−50.3	−32.4	−35.0	2.5

* Apartment complexes of three or more units

Source: Economic Outlook Center, College of Business, Arizona State University

Prospects for the Longer Term

Once past the present period of slow growth, the Arizona economic outlook becomes substantially improved. Again, the key component of the forecast is population growth. According to the U.S. Bureau of the Census, Arizona is projected to lead the nation in the rate of population increase between 1990 and 2000, with a gain of 23.1 percent (Chart 7). The average annual compound rate of increase is 2.1 percent, below the pace of the current year.

Three familiar factors are expected to contribute to population growth in Arizona. First is the persistent draw of climatic conditions and the appeal of the Western lifestyle, primarily to those in the Midwest. In a recent survey of newcomers to Arizona, 65 percent cited reasons other than employment as the primary influence on thcir relocation decision.

Second in importance is the relatively low cost of living in Arizona compared to some other states, particularly California. California has traditionally been a supplier of population to Arizona and other Western states. The lower costs of housing, land and commercial space will be a persistent positive force working on behalf of Arizona's growth during the coming decade.

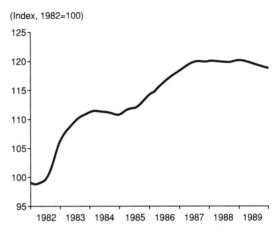

Chart 6
Arizona Index of Leading Economic Indicators

(Index, 1982=100)

Source: Citibank (Arizona) and Economic Outlook Center, College of Business, Arizona State University

The third factor important to growth over the longer run is the state's relative rate of job creation. While the rate of job growth during the next few years is expected to be below Arizona's long-run average, the rate is also expected to be higher than that for several competing states, including Oregon, Washington, Colorado, Texas and even California. Only Nevada is expected to outpace Arizona in new jobs. The Arizona employment growth is tied, of course, to its above-average population growth.

Although considerable research talent has been expended to answer the question of whether jobs draw people or people create jobs, the Arizona experience during the past three decades seems consistent with a simultaneous approach—people come to the state looking for jobs and in the process create a demand for goods and services, which creates employment opportunities.

Most of the new jobs are expected to be of the type that serves local markets, with new positions in government, services and trade but much less activity in manufacturing or finance. Two additional areas of expansion are distribution and transportation, as the state continues to increase in importance as a regional distribution center. Both passenger and cargo activity at Phoenix Sky Harbor International Airport are expected to grow rapidly in the coming decade, continuing a long-established trend.

No discussion of the longer-term outlook for Arizona would be complete without brief mention of the prospects for recovery of the real estate market and the role of the Resolution Trust Corporation (RTC). Local observers are extremely concerned about the possibility that the RTC might attempt to bring a large number of properties to the market in a very short time, thus undercutting property values even more than has already been experienced. In particular, it is argued that dumping office buildings and other commercial facilities would reduce rents and dangerously undermine the profitability of properties that until now had weathered the economic downturn.

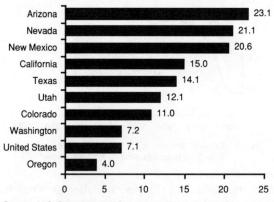

Chart 7
Projected Percent Population Change, 1990–2000

Arizona 23.1
Nevada 21.1
New Mexico 20.6
California 15.0
Texas 14.1
Utah 12.1
Colorado 11.0
Washington 7.2
United States 7.1
Oregon 4.0

0   5   10   15   20   25

Source: U.S. Department of Commerce, Bureau of the Census

Officials with the RTC have sought to calm these fears by emphasizing that one of RTC's objectives is to obtain the maximum value for liquidated properties. In addition, RTC spokespersons have pointed out the numerous legal entanglements that must be unsnarled before many properties can be sold. The lengthy and varying time periods required to gain clear title will likely restrict the RTC from bringing an immediate wave of properties to the market. What is clear, however, is the immense magnitude of holdings that the RTC will eventually bring to the market. Informal estimates range up to $10 billion, approximately equal to the annual value of all sales recorded in the metropolitan Phoenix area in a typical year.

In summary, 1989 represents the lowest point of a period of slower growth for the Arizona economy after spectacular performance during the mid-1980s. 1990 is expected to bring somewhat stronger growth, with job creation of about 2.5 percent, one-half the long-run average of the past two decades. Net migration will continue to be positive, and population will grow by more than 2 percent per year.

In the longer term, this population growth will continue during the next decade, leading to a gain of approximately 1 million, or an increase of nearly 25 percent. While this growth rate is less than that logged during other Arizona expansion periods, it is sufficient to establish Arizona as the fastest-growing state of the 1990s.

Louisiana in the 1990s: A Different Decade

Loren C. Scott

T he theme of this conference declares that the 1990s will be a "different decade." The response of the people of Louisiana is, "Thank God Almighty!"

Seeing the 1980s in our rearview mirror will indeed be a great relief. The past eight years were turbulent and devastating; but the good news is that not only is the Louisiana economy recovering, but also a foundation is being laid for an even better decade ahead.

1973–87: A Roller Coaster Period

That first hill on the roller coaster is always a doozy. The long, exciting ride to the top is followed by the gut-wrenching plunge to the bottom. This is an apt analogy for the 1973–87 period in Louisiana.

Chart 1 shows two distinct phases over the 1973–87 period. First, employment grew rapidly between 1973 and 1981. Louisiana's nonagricultural wage and salary employment grew 4 percent annually, nearly twice the 2.2 percent national average. The cause is straightforward. Louisiana is the country's third-largest producer of oil. In 1973, the wellhead price of Louisiana Sweet Crude was $4 per barrel; by 1981, that price had risen by a factor of nine to $35.45 per barrel.[1] It was a heady, exciting time when even the most adventurous entrepreneur could do no wrong in the Louisiana marketplace.

Unfortunately, there was another side to Louisiana's economic hill. In 1982, the price of crude began to weaken. By 1983, it had fallen to $26–$27 per barrel. Then in 1986, the dramatic drop occurred. At one point in that year, the price of Louisiana petroleum fell to $10.50 per barrel on the spot market.

The effects on the economy were devastating. In oil and gas extraction, employment went from a peak of 101,600 in December 1981 to 50,300 in April 1987.[2] Through the well-known multiplier effect, these layoffs led to workforce reductions in the feeder sectors, such as retail trade, finance, real estate and transportation.

While the oil-price decline was hammering the state's economy, a second serious blow was delivered from another direction. Louisiana has a very large chemical industry; indeed, this sector is responsible for more than 33 percent of the state's value added in manufacturing.[3] Louisiana's chemical industry output is highly concentrated in first-stage, bulk chemicals, and these products typically enjoy a strong foreign demand. For example, in 1984, 22 percent of Louisiana chemical sales were exported.[4]

Chart 1
Louisiana Nonagricultural Wage and Salary Employment
Actual: 1973–89, Projected: 1990–91

Millions Employed

Between 1981 and 1985, the trade-weighted value of the U.S. dollar rose 83 percent, nearly doubling the price of Louisiana chemicals in terms of foreign currencies. Chemical industry sales fell so much that employment was reduced from 33,600 in 1982 to 25,700 in 1987.

The combined hits to these two basic industries—oil and gas extraction and chemicals—sent the Louisiana economy into its deepest and longest recorded recession. For example,

- Between the peak in 1981 and the trough in 1987, the state lost 146,900 nonagricultural wage and salary jobs—a 9-percent reduction in the work force.
- At one point in early 1987, the statewide unemployment rate reached 14.5 percent.
- In 1986, *nominal* personal income fell for the first time since these figures became available at the state level.
- Real per capita income—arguably the best measure of the welfare of the individual citizen—fell in five of the seven years between 1981 and 1987. Louisiana's rank among the states dropped from 32nd in 1982 to 46th in 1987.
- The state government—heavily dependent on mineral-related sources for revenues—ran deficits in four of the five fiscal years between 1983–84

and 1987–88. These deficits totaled $957 million for a general appropriations budget that is typically around $4 billion per year.

- Louisiana's bond rating dropped to Baa, which is one step above junk bonds and the lowest rating of any state bonds in the country.
- In 1987, Louisiana's population fell by 1.1 percent—the first decline since World War II. Population declined again in 1988—this time by 0.9 percent—as citizens looked for better opportunities elsewhere.

Is there any wonder that Louisiana citizens will be glad to put the 1980s behind them?

Recent Changes and Forecasts for 1990–91
If this story ended in 1987, it would be a depressing story indeed. But there is good news. Beginning in October 1987, the Louisiana economy began to grow again and has now experienced employment growth every month for two consecutive years. The growth rate has not been spectacular—about two-thirds that of the national average—but it has been consistently positive.

The recovery has been generated largely by the huge drop in the U.S. dollar, the value of which is back down to where it was before the 1981–85 run-up. Louisiana's chemical firms are enjoying a significant resurgence in foreign demand for their products and have responded by announcing more than $2 billion in plant expansions to meet these foreign orders.[5] More than 8,000 industrial construction jobs were created between 1987 and 1989 to build new plants and to expand existing ones.

The forecasting team at Louisiana State University projects that the recovery that began in late 1987 will continue for the next two years.[6] Table 1 shows some details from that forecast, including growth rates in nonagricultural wage and salary employment for broadly defined sectors. Table 1 illustrates actual data for 1988, estimated figures for 1989 (based on eight months of data) and projections for 1990 and 1991.

The key to Louisiana's immediate economic future lies in its manufacturing sector. We project 5,200 new manufacturing jobs over the next two years. This growth is expected to be *export-fueled* as our chemical, paper and apparel industries enjoy the benefits of a weak U.S. dollar.

As mentioned above, several plants have announced planned expansions over the next two years, a factor that will generate further growth in Louisiana's construction industry. The mining sector, which is primarily oil and gas extraction in Louisiana, is projected to grow weakly. At least it is not expected to be the drag on the economy that it was in the early 1980s. Despite higher oil prices recently, we see extreme reluctance to return to the oil fields in a big way because of concern about OPEC quota cheating and other uncertainties about downward pressures on oil prices.

Projected general growth in Louisiana's basic industries will naturally lead to additional employment in the feeder sectors of retail trade, services and transportation, communications and public utilities (TCPU). Despite nice gains in these areas, the finance, insurance and real estate (FIRE) sector will still experience serious declines. Louisiana has more than 40 thrift institutions that do not meet the minimum capital requirements under the savings and loan bailout legislation. These thrifts will be either closed or merged with other financial institutions over the next 18 months. Also, bank merger activity is still alive and well in our state. We forecast that the finance sector will lose about 1,900 jobs over the next two years because of these adjustments.

Finally, the government sector has been a major job drain on the Louisiana economy, primarily because of massive declines in state government employment. Under Governor Buddy Roemer's administration, state government employment declined by 6,100 jobs between 1987 and 1989 alone. Because of court-mandated expansions in the corrections area and new federal funds for the welfare and health care sectors, state government employment should rise

Table 1
Louisiana Wage and Salary Employment
(Percent change)

Sector	1988	1989*	1990**	1991**
Mining	3.3	.9	.4	.3
Construction	3.4	6.5	1.6	1.2
Manufacturing	3.4	1.3	1.3	1.7
TCPU***	2.3	2.2	1.9	1.9
Trade	−.5	1.0	1.0	1.3
FIRE****	−2.4	−2.4	−2.1	−.5
Services	2.5	1.0	1.5	1.5
Government	.4	0	.8	.7
Total	1.2	1.0	1.0	1.2

* Estimates based on eight months of data
** Projections
*** Transportation, Communication and Public Utilities
**** Finance, Insurance and Real Estate

gradually over the next two years and begin to contribute to, rather than detract from, state employment growth.

As can be seen along the bottom of Table 1, the LSU forecasters project that the Louisiana economy will grow by 1 percent in 1990 and 1.2 percent in 1991. Those growth rates are about two-thirds to three-fourths of that projected for the national economy, which suggests that we are recovering, but work remains to be done.

Fundamental Changes Occurring

Fortunately, evidence indicates that *fundamental* changes are occurring. As so often has happened in the economic history of the United States, when a crisis occurs, capitalists make necessary adjustments to protect themselves from a repeat of past mistakes. One of Louisiana's mistakes was to have an undiversified, oil-dependent economy. So, when oil prices collapsed between 1981 and 1987, our economy fell like an unopened parachute.

Now there is clear evidence of marginal moves toward diversification. Major shipyards, such as Avondale and McDermott, once concentrated on constructing offshore platforms and ships and barges to service the offshore drilling industry. Now these firms have diversified into the national defense arena and are building ships and submarines for the Navy. An apparel industry has blossomed in the state, creating 2,800 jobs in just the past two years.

Perhaps even more important than the diversification moves has been the expression of the people through their state government that they are ready to do things differently. Long a stronghold of populism, Louisiana has taken several significant steps toward a pro-business environment—steps that would never have been taken in the 1960s, 1970s or early 1980s. Consider the following:

- *Unemployment Compensation.* Louisiana's unemployment compensation (UC) benefits were once the highest in the South and among the most liberal in the country. The result—Louisiana levied some of the highest UC taxes on business in the country. Those benefits have been reduced and are now among the most conservative in the United States, and the UC debt accrued during the recession has been refinanced to lower this business tax burden significantly.
- *Workmen's Compensation.* Legislation was passed to move from jury trials to hearings before administrative law judges—making the procedure much less adversarial for business.
- *Adoption of Chapter 9 of the Uniform Commercial Code.* Among the 50 states, only Louisiana had not adopted this legislation, which establishes the procedural aspects of contracts. Louisiana is now in line with the other states.

- *Repeal of the Prevailing Wage Law.* Wages paid on state construction contracts are now based on market wages and not on the union scale prevailing in the area.
- *Tort Reform.* A products liability bill was passed that has become a model for other states. The "state-of-the-art" defense is now part of Louisiana law, which will reduce the threat of future suits against businesses.
- *Budget Reforms.* Businesslike procedures for establishing the state budget are now part of Louisiana law. There is a Revenue Forecasting Conference that establishes the state revenue forecast each year— removing that process from the deficit-creating political arena. All measures are designed to make the state budget more stable and predictable.
- *TIME.* In October 1989, Louisiana citizens overwhelmingly passed the Transportation Infrastructure Model for Economic Development (TIME) bill. This $1.4 billion program will—among other things—(1) construct four-lane highways connecting all major cities in Louisiana (Chart 2), (2) pump $75 million into the New Orleans Airport to make it eligible to become a regional hub, and (3) inject $100 million into the New Orleans Port to bring it into the modern age of containerized shipping.
- *Children First Act.* Designed to upgrade K–12 education in Louisiana, this bill pumps more dollars into elementary and secondary education. Among its planks is a schedule of teacher raises of 5 percent, 7 percent and 7 percent a year over a three-year period. Two of these pay raises have already been awarded.
- *Campaign Finance Legislation.* Perhaps the nation's toughest campaign-finance law was passed in 1988. This law limits contributions to statewide races to $5,000 per individual contributor and $10,000 per political action committee. For local races, the limits are $1,000 and $2,000, respectively. This legislation is perhaps the state's most powerful signal to the rest of the country about its citizens' expectations regarding integrity in state government.

This legislative package is remarkable in both its length and depth. It represents a very real statement by the people of Louisiana that they want the 1990s to be a "different decade."

Challenges Ahead

While the progress made so far has certainly been noteworthy, fundamental problems still exist in Louisiana. Louisiana's tax structure, when compared to other states' tax structures, still remains relatively punitive toward business. For example, in 1985 business paid 22 percent of the Louisiana tax bill. The

Chart 2
Existing Interstates and Roads to Become Four Lanes

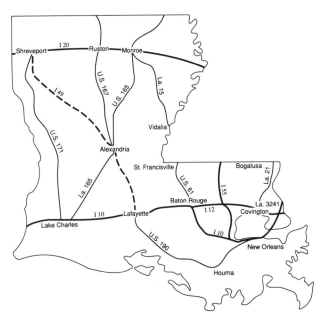

Southeastern state average for business was 13.2 percent, and the closest state to Louisiana was Alabama at 17.7 percent.[7] Because of a heavy reliance on sales taxes at the local level, the tax structure is also more regressive than it should be. Tax reform that shifts some of the burden from business to individuals and from the poor to the rich is still badly needed.

The Children First Act has begun to address the education problem in the K–12 grades, but higher education suffers from both funding and governance problems. A poorly funded higher education system will be a major deterrent in attracting the futuristic industries of the 1990s to Louisiana.

Still, it is encouraging that many Louisiana citizens and government officials recognize that these problems need to be addressed. In fact, Governor Roemer has stated publicly that the resolution of these two issues will be center stage in his legislative agenda over the next two years.

Recently, the U.S. Census Bureau made population forecasts for each of the 50 states for the 1990s. Louisiana's population grew by 561,000 in the 1970s and by 307,000 in the 1980s. The Census Bureau predicts that Louisiana will grow by only *3,000* people in the 1990s.[8] Their reason for this uncommonly pessimistic forecast was that the Louisiana economy will perform so poorly relative to other states in the next decade that out-migration to better state economies will almost totally offset any natural growth in the Louisiana population.

To at least some extent, this conclusion is based on the notion that things will not change in Louisiana. Had this article been written during the 1983–85 period, I would have been inclined to agree with the Census projection. But in the past two years, Louisiana citizens have shown a willingness to make substantive changes. Changes are already being made that could make the Census forecast for our state one of the worst the Bureau ever made. These changes are designed to make the 1990s truly a different decade for Louisiana.

Notes

[1]   *Center for Energy Studies, Louisiana State University, Baton Rouge, La.*

[2]   *Louisiana Department of Labor, revised data, Mimeograph.*

[3]   1986 Annual Survey of Manufacturers, Geographic Area Series, *Bureau of Census, U.S. Department of Commerce, July 1988, pp. 3–20.*

[4]   1984 Annual Survey of Manufactures, Origin of Exports of Manufactured Products, *Bureau of Census, U.S. Department of Commerce, August 1987, p. 25. For a detailed analysis of the Louisiana chemical industry, see Loren C. Scott,* The Chemical Industry in Louisiana, *Louisiana Chemical Association, Baton Rouge, La., September 1989.*

[5]   *Virginia Simons, "Louisiana Industrial Expansion," Mimeograph by The Port of South Louisiana, LaPlace, La., August 31, 1989.*

[6]   *Loren C. Scott, James A. Richardson, and A.M.M. Jamal, "The Louisiana Economic Outlook: 1990 and 1991," College of Business, Louisiana State University, October 1989.*

[7]   Louisiana's Fiscal Alternatives: Finding Permanent Solutions to Recurring Budget Crises, *ed. James A. Richardson (Baton Rouge, La.: Louisiana State University Press, 1988):160.*

[8]   Projections of the Population of the States, by Age, Sex, and Race: 1988 to 2010, *U.S. Department of Commerce, Bureau of the Census, Series 8–25, No. 1017.*

The New Mexico Economy

M. Brian McDonald

I am very happy to be here this morning for a couple of reasons. One is that I am pretty confident that I am speaking to a group that knows that New Mexico is one of the 50 states. Our state tourism department continues to get hundreds of calls from potential visitors inquiring whether you need a passport or if you can drink the water or what the local exchange rate is.

Second, I am happy because I do not find myself among a group of economists who are probably going to be talking about the economy in optimistic terms. Certainly after listening to the first two talks and knowing something about what is to come, I think New Mexico's recent economic performance has probably been the best of the five Southwestern states we are discussing today. Within New Mexico I am probably referred to as someone who is gloomy and doomy, but this morning I will play a different role, which is nice.

Let me start with some basic socioeconomic statistics about New Mexico (Table 1). New Mexico has a small economy. Our total nonagricultural employment in 1988 was 540,000. (Lee McPheters mentioned that Arizona created that many new jobs in the last 10 years.) Our population is a little more than 1.5 million. The state has a relatively high unemployment rate; some areas in the state have high structural unemployment. Personal income is about $20 billion. Per capita income ranks 45th among the 50 states and is only 76 percent of the U.S. average. So, New Mexico's economy is a relatively small economy and also a relatively poor one, measured by per capita income.

Table 2 provides information about the structure of the New Mexico economy, showing where our jobs are by sector. I would like to point out a couple of things. New Mexico has a very large government sector. (Table 2 shows local, state and federal government employment.) In 1988, government employment accounted for 26 percent of New Mexico's jobs. Nationally, government jobs account for 16.4 percent of total employment. So, we have a very large government sector.

In contrast, we have a very small manufacturing sector. About 7 percent of our jobs are in manufacturing. Not many other states have such a small manufacturing base.

Table 1
New Mexico Statistical Overview

Population	1.507 million	• As of July 1, 1988 • Population grew 1.75 percent in the 1980s
Nonagricultural Employment	540,000	• As of 1988 • New Mexico experienced 1.89-percent growth in employment in the 1980s.
Unemployment Rate	7.1 percent	• As of the first half of 1989
Personal Income	$20.008 billion	• As of the first quarter of 1989
Per Capita Income	$12,488	• As of 1988 • New Mexico ranks 45th among the 50 states. • Per capita income in New Mexico is 76 percent that of the U.S. average.

Table 2 shows New Mexico's statistics for both 1981 and 1988 to highlight what has happened in the state's mining sector. Our mining employment peaked in 1981 at about 31,000 jobs, which represented about 6.6 percent of our total jobs. We have lost basically half the jobs in our mining sector, which now represents less than 3 percent of our total employment. So, we have had a major structural change in our economy.

In our service sector, however, we have had very strong growth. Employment in this sector has grown from about 20 percent of the jobs in 1981 to about 24 percent of the jobs in 1988. Charts 1 and 2 show New Mexico employment growth by sector from the second quarter of 1989.

I want to focus a bit more on our government sector. While it is large—in fact, probably one of the largest in any state—it is even larger than Table 2 shows. If you look at our published data on federal employment from our Department of Labor, you will find the 30,400 jobs listed under civilian employment broken out between defense- and nondefense-related employment (Table 3). Although the data report 30,400 jobs, a lot of other employment in New Mexico relates directly to the federal government. For example, New Mexico's four military installations employ more than 22,000 service men and

Table 2
New Mexico and U.S. Nonagricultural Employment by Sector— 1981, 1988
(In thousands)

Sector	New Mexico 1981	New Mexico 1988	United States 1988
Trade	105.983	130.375	25,350.0
(Percent of total)	22.3	24.1	23.9
Services	94.142	127.917	25,460.0
(Percent of total)	19.8	23.7	24.0
Government	125.333	140.800	17,390.0
(Percent of total)	26.5	26.1	16.4
Manufacturing	34.333	39.883	19,540.0
(Percent of total)	7.2	7.4	18.4
Mining	31.200	15.358	730.0
(Percent of total)	6.6	2.8	.7
Construction	33.258	30.192	5,290.0
(Percent of total)	7.0	5.6	5.0
TCPU*	29.208	28.850	5,580.0
(Percent of total)	6.1	5.3	5.3
Finance	21.508	27.017	6,680.0
(Percent of total)	4.5	5.0	6.3
Total	475.465	540.392	106,000.0

Sources: New Mexico Department of Labor and U.S. Department of Labor

* TCPU = Transportation, Communications and Public Utilities

women. We have two large national laboratories. Sandia National Laboratory, which is operated by AT&T in Albuquerque, is classified in the services sector because AT&T is a private company. Los Alamos National Laboratory, north of Albuquerque, has more than 8,000 employees. The University of California operates Los Alamos, so the lab is classified as state government. Then we have

---

Table 3
The Federal Government and the New Mexico Economy
(June 1988)

Military Employment*	22,717
Federal Civilian Employment	
—Defense-related	10,200
—Nondefense-related	20,200
Private Defense Contractors	
—Sandia National Laboratory (Services sector)	7,503
—Los Alamos National Laboratory (State government sector)	8,000
—Honeywell, Inc. (Manufacturing sector)	2,600
— BDM Corporation (Services sector)	850
—Other on defense installations	7,268
Total Federal-Related Employment	79,338
(As a percentage of total employment)**	14.4

*   Includes active duty, National Guard and reserves, according to the U.S. Bureau of Economic Analysis estimate for 1986.
**   Includes military employment.

Sources: *The Social and Economic Impact of the Department of Energy on the State of New Mexico, 1987 FY*, selected resource impact statements from New Mexico's major defense installations and Bureau of Business and Economic Research, University of New Mexico.

Albuquerque's major manu-
facturer, Honeywell, which is
primarily a defense contrac-
tor, making avionics products. BDM corporation, the
large government engineering services firm, has its
western regional headquar-
ters in Albuquerque. More
than 7,000 other private-sector jobs exist on defense installations in New Mexico. Add
all of these together and you
get almost 80,000 jobs in New
Mexico that are directly
funded by the federal government, and that number is a
little more than 14 percent of

Chart 1
**New Mexico Employment Growth
by Sector (1989:2)**

Percent change, year over year

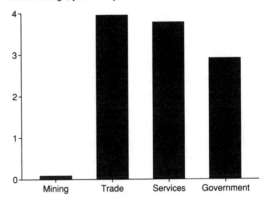

our jobs. If you count employment in state and local government, almost one-
third of our jobs are in the government sector.

Reviewing New Mexico's economic performance, Table 4 presents the
state's nonagricultural em-
ployment growth rates from
1950 to 1989, and Chart 3
focuses on 1980–89. In 1989,
one can see that since the
lows of 1986 and 1987 when
the state had virtually no
growth after the oil price falls,
New Mexico's economy has
begun to recover. The state's
job growth is now about 2.5
percent. Much of the growth
is in manufacturing. We have
also had strong growth in
tourism. We had much
stronger personal income
growth over the past few
years, which has helped the
trade and service sectors. New

Chart 2
**New Mexico Employment Growth
by Sector (1989:2)**

Percent change, year over year

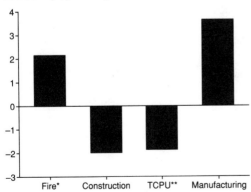

* Finance, Insurance and Real Estate
**Transportation, Communication and Public Utilities

Mexico's population continues to grow at about double the national rate, and school teaching is a growth industry in the state.

Looking at the 1980s, one can see the very slow growth early in the decade caused by two national recessions, the first oil price collapse and the collapse of the state's uranium and mining industries. In 1982, we see the first employment decline in New Mexico since 1961. In contrast to New Mexico's slow growth in the 1980s, the state's annual growth rate in the 1970s averaged almost 5 percent per year. In the 1980s, we reached that growth rate in only one year, 1984. So, the 1980s have been a relatively slow period of growth for New Mexico, although more recently growth is resuming.

One example of New Mexico's new growth is in personal income. Chart 4 shows how personal income is beginning to grow again in the state. This year the farm economy is improving, although it is a small sector in New Mexico. Our farmers seem to have avoided the effects of the drought, but they benefited from the higher prices. Wages and salaries are growing again. In 1986–88, we had very slow personal income growth, which had big implications for the state's general-fund revenues, 65 percent of which now come from gross receipts tax (our sales tax) and income taxes. We had big declines in oil and gas revenue as well.

Chart 5 examines employment growth in New Mexico and the United States. In the early 1980s, New Mexico was outperforming the U.S. economy. In fact, throughout the 1970s New Mexico outperformed the U.S. economy. In the mid-

Table 4
New Mexico and U.S. Nonagricultural Employment Growth Rates*, 1950–89 (Percent)

Period	New Mexico	United States
1950–60	4.54	1.83
1960–70	2.20	2.72
1970–80	4.75	2.46
1980–89	1.89	2.10

* Compound annual rates of change

Sources: U.S. Department of Labor and New Mexico Department of Labor.

Chart 3
New Mexico Nonagricultural Employment—Percent Change, 1980–89

Annual percent change

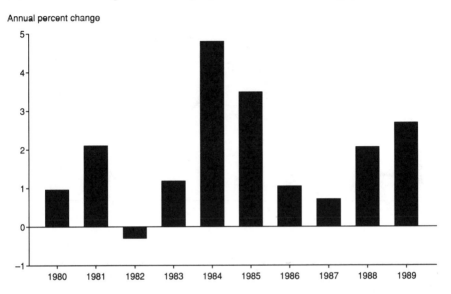

Chart 4
New Mexico Personal Income—Percent Change, 1980–89

Annual percent change

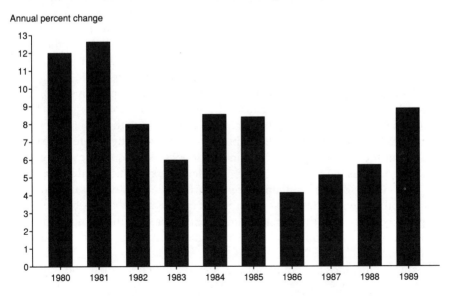

Chart 5
Employment Growth—United States and New Mexico, 1980–89

Annual percent change

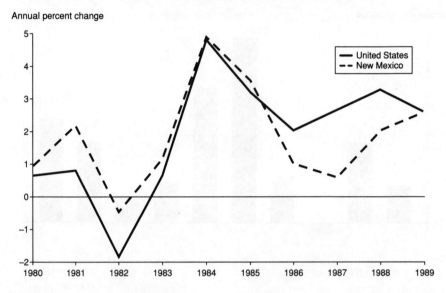

1980s, New Mexico and the United States began to perform at about the same rate. From 1986 to 1989, New Mexico's economy grew less than the U.S. economy. This is a very strange situation for New Mexico. You would have to look to the early 1960s to find that situation in the past. But with the oil price decline in 1986, the state's economy grew very slowly. Now in 1989, the state is climbing closer to the national rates. The reasons for this are a combination of New Mexico's doing better and the United States slowing down a bit.

Chart 6 reviews the situation in some of the state's metropolitan areas. New Mexico has three metropolitan statistical areas (MSAs). Albuquerque is New Mexico's largest MSA and accounts for about 43 percent of the jobs in the state. So, it is a major employment center. Albuquerque consistently outgrew the state throughout the 1980s. However, beginning in 1988, Albuquerque's economy has slowed to less than the state's rate. Lee McPheters mentioned that Phoenix and Tucson are growing less than the rest of Arizona. New Mexico's urban areas are currently growing a little less than the rest of the state. Within Albuquerque, there is a correction in the construction sector. There is virtually no manufacturing growth in Albuquerque; the state's manufacturing growth is outside Albuquerque.

Santa Fe includes the county of Los Alamos, which is where the National

Laboratory is located. There has been virtually no growth there for the past two years. About the only positive thing in the Santa Fe area is tourism and a lot of Californians coming to purchase real estate. In the Santa Fe and Taos area, there is a lot of anecdotal evidence about people who commute to Los Angeles on Monday and return on Friday to spend the weekend in Santa Fe.

The one urban area in New Mexico that is doing well is Las Cruces, which is in the Dallas Fed region. It is very close to El Paso. There is strong growth in retail trade and construction in the Las Cruces area.

I want to focus on three issues that are important for the outlook of New Mexico's economy. First is the link with the federal government. I have already talked about the importance of the federal government in terms of jobs, but we will now look at it with a more historical perspective. Chart 7 plots New Mexico employment levels and real federal spending within the state. You can see a very strong correlation between federal spending and employment levels in New Mexico. In fact, in the early 1980s federal spending fell slightly in real terms. The Reagan administration cut much of the federal research for unconventional energy, which was being done at our laboratories. That also coincided with the first oil price decline. Strong growth in federal spending, particularly for the Strategic Defense Initiative (SDI) program, caused a miniboom in the mid-1980s. New Mexico is second only to California in the dollar amount of SDI research

Chart 6
Employment Growth—New Mexico and Metropolitan Areas, 1983–89

Annual percent change

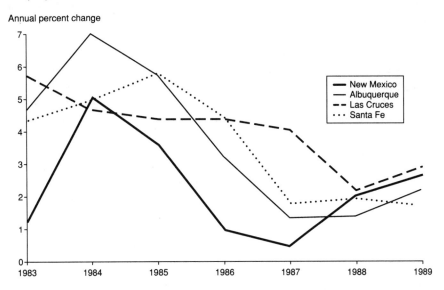

Chart 7
New Mexico Employment and Federal Spending, 1967–87

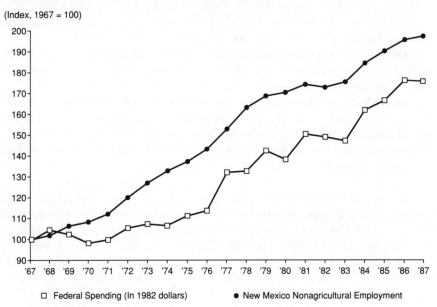

(Index, 1967 = 100)

□ Federal Spending (In 1982 dollars)   ● New Mexico Nonagricultural Employment

money, principally used at Los Alamos' National Laboratory. Federal spending flattened in 1987, and as best as we can tell it has stayed at about that level. The outlook for federal spending is obviously very key to the New Mexico economic outlook.

Chart 8 gives a little more detail about what has happened to New Mexico's mining sector. New Mexico has a diversified mining sector—oil, natural gas, coal, copper, potash, molybdenum and uranium. In the early 1980s, however, almost all of the sectors—perhaps with the exception of coal—headed south. Oil and gas employment peaked at about 15,000, and now it is about 8,000. In metal mining, New Mexico had about 9,000 uranium workers in the late 1970s. Chevron and Homestake are closing the last two major uranium mines in November 1989, and New Mexico will have virtually no uranium activity. In the late 1970s, New Mexico was probably the number one world producer of uranium. Extractive industries are still important to New Mexico's economy. We do not see any recovery in any of these industries throughout the mid-1990s.

Chart 9 depicts construction in Albuquerque. There was a boom in the mid-1980s in many urban centers of the country in housing construction, particularly apartment construction. Single-family housing construction was strong for four or five years. In 1988, single-family housing construction fell about 25 percent, and it has fallen about another 25 percent in 1989. Currently, there is virtually no multifamily housing construction in New Mexico. In 1989, there was one 300-unit facility built. Vacancy rates are about 12 percent to 14 percent. Albuquerque has a three-year to four-year supply of apartments. Construction has been New Mexico's weakest sector for the past three years. The state has lost perhaps 20 percent to 25 percent of construction jobs in the past three years. We think 1989 will be the bottom for that, with perhaps little improvement in 1990 and 1991.

Let me turn now to the outlook for New Mexico. Chart 10 is a quarterly forecast that I plotted against a forecast of U.S. employment, which in this graph is a forecast by Data Resources, and they are a little pessimistic compared to the consensus. Chart 11 is a quarterly forecast of personal income growth in the United States and New Mexico. Chart 12 shows a quarterly forecast of employment growth in New Mexico and its three MSAs.

In 1990, New Mexico nonagricultural employment should grow about 2 percent, after about 2.5 percent in 1989. So, growth is slowing a bit. In 1991, nonagricultural employment should grow about 1 percent, although that is predicated on a fairly substantial slowdown in the national economy. In 1990, we are expecting a little slower growth in manufacturing, which has been a very

Chart 8
New Mexico Mining Employment, 1965–88
Metal, Nonmetal and Oil and Gas

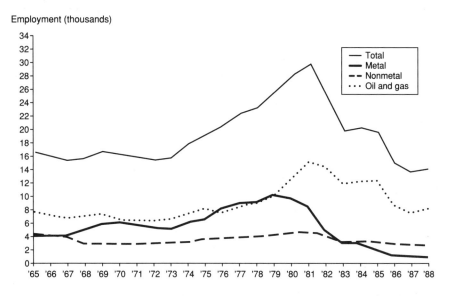

Employment (thousands)

Chart 9
Albuquerque Study Area Housing Permits, 1980–88

Number of permits

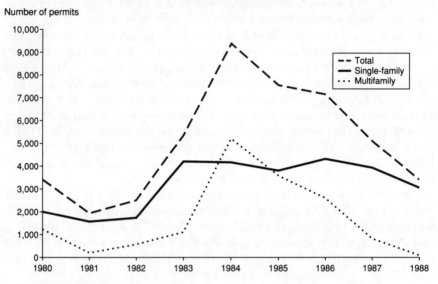

Source: *Socioeconomic Projections for Albuquerque, 1980–2000*, City of Albuquerque, Planning
         Department, July 1989.

strong sector in New Mexico for the past two years. A lot of the growth has been
due to a single manufacturer. Because of New Mexico's small manufacturing
base, the state's numbers jump when it gets one new manufacturer. A bus
manufacturing plant in the Roswell area had a major expansion, hiring about
1,000 new workers in 1987 and 1988. We do not anticipate that kind of a new
manufacturer in 1990 or 1991, but we still expect manufacturing to be a strong
sector in 1990. There are many small new manufacturers moving into the
Albuquerque area, particularly Rio Rancho, where two Japanese companies are
hiring 60 people to 80 people with the hope of expanding.

The forecast that 1991 will have slower growth is caused primarily by higher
inflation and what that does to real disposable income within the state and what
it does to our trade and service sectors.

Let me conclude by talking about a few long-term issues for the New Mexico
economy, some of which are positive and some of which are negative. I think
the strongest positive for the New Mexico economy in the 1990s will be our labor
force growth. Our population continues to grow at about double the national
rate. It is growing at a little less than 2 percent now. We have a young population,

Chart 10
Employment Growth—United States and New Mexico (1987:3–1991:2)

Percent change, year over year

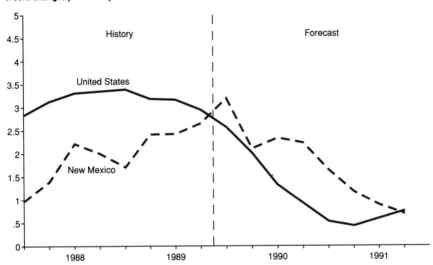

Chart 11
Personal Income Growth—United States and New Mexico (1987:3–1991:2)

Percent change, year over year

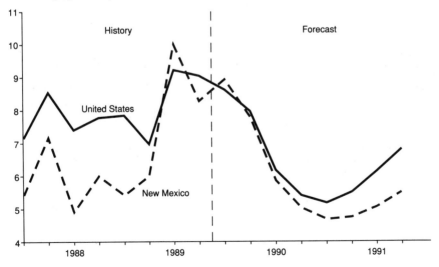

and we will have a labor force available in the 1990s. Many states will have a shortage of labor supply in the 1990s. If it is a high-cost area, the state will have difficulty getting people to migrate there. In fact, many of the new manufacturers and other businesses that have come to Albuquerque have indicated that the labor force was a factor in their decision to move here. New Mexico's labor force also tends to be less mobile than the labor forces in other areas. Much of the Hispanic population has been in the state for years. They are very traditional and tied to the land. New businesses find in New Mexico not only a labor force but also a labor force with low turnover.

Tourism will also continue to be a growth area for New Mexico. We will have to stop selling our natural resources from out of the ground and sell another type of our natural resources—that is, our mountains, our ski industry and our quality of life. And this is happening. Certainly with our sparsely populated areas, we have lots of room and beautiful vistas and a high quality of life.

Perhaps a negative issue for New Mexico is federal spending. We are not looking for any substantial negative effects. Much of the federal spending in New Mexico is research-and-development related—nuclear weapons, "Star Wars," verification for environmental cleanup. It is not procurement contracts. We think that procurement contracts will be more cyclical, although this area is a major

Chart 12
Employment Growth—New Mexico and Metropolitan Areas
(1987:3–1991:2)

Percent change, year over year

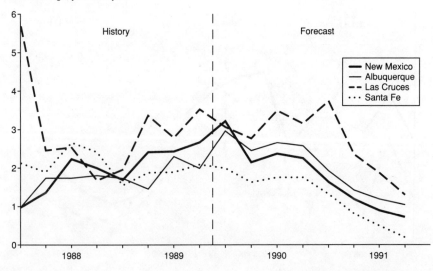

risk for New Mexico in the 1990s. We certainly do not expect it to be a growth sector, and for that reason New Mexico must look to other sectors, such as manufacturing, tourism and business services, for growth.

There are some positives in the federal area. In the base-closure exercise that is currently going on, New Mexico comes out a net winner. We will probably gain 2,000 to 2,500 military jobs, some in the Albuquerque area and some in Clovis, which is on the Texas–New Mexico border in the Panhandle area. We are not exactly sure when those jobs are coming, probably sometime in the early 1990s.

Finally, New Mexico is working very hard to diversify its economy. The state realizes it has a problem with its dependence on federal spending. Certainly the state's small manufacturing base is an area that New Mexico needs to work on and is working on, with some success for the past two years. New Mexico has a lot to offer in terms of cost of living, labor force and water. Certainly compared to Arizona, New Mexico has a plentiful water supply. So, New Mexico is an attractive place for businesses to locate, perhaps with the exception of our geographic isolation—New Mexico is far from major markets. But for those businesses that do not have heavy transportation costs, that will not be a factor.

In summary, New Mexico has an economically small and relatively poor regional economy. The state's leading economic sector is the federal government. New Mexico also has a diversified mining industry; significant tourism that includes recreation, arts and crafts and Native American and Hispanic cultures; and a small manufacturing base that represents 7 percent of total employment.

New Mexico's economy performed poorly in the 1980s because of the collapse of its mining industries. Current economic growth, however, has climbed back to the national average and is led by strong expansion in manufacturing and tourism.

The Albuquerque MSA accounts for 43.5 percent of total state employment. Until recently, the city's economy had outperformed the state's economy. The current slowdown in Albuquerque's growth can be traced to an ongoing correction in the construction sector, weak manufacturing and a slowdown in federal defense spending within the city.

In the short run, analysts expect New Mexico's economy to grow at the national average. Projections for 1990 place growth at 2.2 percent and growth in personal income at 6.8 percent. In the long run, factors clouding New Mexico's future are an overreliance on defense spending and mineral extraction, as well as the state's small manufacturing sector.

The Oklahoma Economy: The Next Year and the Next Decade

Larkin Warner

T his discussion will elaborate on three conclusions. First, during 1990 the Oklahoma economy will improve slightly with key real income and output variables not growing more than 1 percent. Second, the next major national recession—when it comes—may not be quite as serious a problem for Oklahoma as it will be for other regions. Third, state employment will grow, but at a rate somewhat less than the relatively turgid rate of the U.S. economy during the 1990s.

These are not exciting predictions; they suggest a partial return to underlying conditions influencing Oklahoma economic growth in the 1960s and early 1970s. But this partial return will be in the context of national and international economic systems, which are—as the theme of this conference asserts—rather different from the past.

Before proceeding further, I will note some of Oklahoma's basic economic dimensions on the eve of the 1990s.

- The state's 3.24 million population is 1.3 percent of the U.S. total; despite declines since 1984, this figure remains 200,000 above the 1980 level.
- Fifty-two percent of Oklahoma's population lives in the Oklahoma City and Tulsa metropolitan statistical areas (MSAs); another 11 percent lives in five counties containing Lawton, Enid, Ponca City, Muskogee and Stillwater.
- Per capita personal income is 81 percent of the U.S. average—down from 99 percent in 1982, but about the same relative level as in the 1960s and early 1970s.
- Gross state product (GSP) is about $55 billion. Oil and agriculture, the state's historic bellwether industries, contribute 14 percent of GSP and 8 percent of employment.

- Nonfarm wage and salary employment of 1.14 million is down about 80,000 from its 1982 average, but it has edged upward since mid-1986.
- Largely as a result of distressed economic conditions, prices are relatively low in Oklahoma; a weighted-average cost-of-living index for seven of the state's major cities stands at 94.2 percent of the U.S. all-city average.[1]

The Next Year

The consensus about the "soft landing scenario" for the U.S. economy in 1990 is so generally held that it almost gives one pause. Could the herd instinct of the economic forecasters be leading them to overlook the likelihood of very near-term trouble? Probably not. Remember that this soft landing forecast is certainly not wildly optimistic. National growth will be slow, and it is unlikely that unemployment rates will fall any lower. In fact, a mild recession is so close to the soft landing that the forecaster who misses by a tad can be forgiven easily. But until economic data indicate otherwise, forecasts of small regional sub-economies should assume modest growth impulses flowing from the national system over the next year.

What are the large-scale, econometric, model-based forecasts indicating for 1990 in Oklahoma? The big annual and quarterly state models located at Oklahoma State University's Office of Business and Economic Research now use national variables from DRI/McGraw–Hill. Using a national forecast of real gross national product (GNP) growth of 1.7 percent, fourth quarter of 1989 to fourth quarter of 1990, the Oklahoma State University (OSU) quarterly model generates a growth of 1.4 percent in Oklahoma's real gross state product.[2] The WEFA Group is forecasting Oklahoma nonagricultural employment beginning to grow at roughly the same rate as its national counterpart during early 1990.[3]

A forecast of slight growth during Oklahoma's next year is certainly reasonable in light of its performance since 1986. Oklahoma's economy crashed from mid-1982 through mid-1986 and experienced an anemic recovery lasting into the autumn of 1989. A glimmer of optimism in 1984 waned in 1985 even before the second big negative oil shock of 1986. As expected, the four-year recession was associated with numerous painful corrective adjustments, some of which will still be in process in the early 1990s. However, these adjustments cannot continue to be a problem indefinitely in an environment of steady national economic growth. After dropping 12 percent, or 155,000, between the peak in May 1982 to the trough in July 1986, state nonagricultural employment stabilized during the last half of 1986 and the first half of 1987. Then, during the 25-month period from August 1987 through August 1989, nonagricultural employment exceeded the level recorded 12 months earlier for every month except July 1989, when the estimate was down by only 100. The only thing remarkable about this year-to-year growth pattern in the monthly employment statistics is its consistency; the mean year-to-year employment change during these 25 months was only 1.4 percent. With slower growth nationally, it is likely that Oklahoma's employment will grow even more slowly during 1990—but there is no reason to expect a decline.

Four other pieces of data are worth mentioning as support for the reasonableness of slight Oklahoma growth in 1990. First, Southwestern Bell and the University of Oklahoma's Center for Economic and Management Research have created a General Business Index. Although well below its peak in 1981–82, the index rose fairly steadily between the second quarter of 1986 and the first quarter of 1989. However, data for the second quarter of 1989 indicate a slight drop in this composite index and thus should restrain any ebullience about 1990.[4] Second, current data on state government tax receipts are consistent with continued modest expansion. The first two months of fiscal 1990 show general revenue fund receipts up 1.5 percent from a year earlier.[5] Third, the Mid-America Survey of purchasing managers for Oklahoma projects show Oklahoma growth during 1989.[6] Fourth, the Oklahoma Department of Commerce's October 1989 news release summarizing a set of state economic indicators emphasizes mixed performance of key variables.[7]

Implicit in the slow-growth forecast for the Oklahoma economy during the next year is the assumption that there will be little change in internal economic structure. Agriculture, mining, manufacturing and federal government employment may be viewed as the state's principal economic base, selling goods, services and entitlements outside the state in return for an inflow of payments. In terms of direct employment, this basic component exhibited very little change between mid-1987 and mid-1989 and is unlikely to change much in 1990. Farm employment will continue to hover around 50,000. Durable manufacturing jobs will edge beyond the 100,000 level as long as the dollar does not rise dramatically, and nondurable manufacturing may move toward the 65,000 range. Mining appears to have stabilized at about 45,000 jobs and may not drop much, even though recent OPEC actions suggest that Oklahoma premium prices for crude oil will not be maintained.[8] Federal employment is stuck at about 50,000 jobs, and there is nothing to indicate big shifts during the 1990 federal fiscal year.

Oklahoma and the First Recession of the 1990s

Although the Federal Reserve seems to be doing a superb stabilization job, few are espousing a kind of post-modern view of macroeconomic policy in which the business cycle is dead. There is much uncertainty about what lies beyond 1990. Forecasts of a 1991 recovery from the 1990 growth recession are based strongly on a "return-to-trend" view of the economy—always a safe but question-begging forecast.

But a recession will come, and there is concern that it will be of above-average severity due to the economy's extensive accumulation of debt. However different the 1990s will be, surely the 1980s will be distinguished by future generations as the "decade of debt." The ratio of nonfinancial debt to GNP hovered around 1.35 to 1.4 throughout the 1960s and 1970s, but the ratio moved upward rapidly in the 1980s to 1.81 in the first quarter of 1989. With an unusually highly leveraged corporate sector and a debt-laden household sector, the next recession could unwind rapidly.

Oklahoma is probably not a very highly leveraged state. It is the site of few major corporate home offices. One exception, Phillips Petroleum Co., seems to be working its way out of the over-leveraged position in which it found itself as it fended off hostile takeovers. Of course, much other debt throughout the state has simply vanished. To the extent that debt structure affects regional differentials during this next recession, Oklahoma may fare relatively well. A low level of cyclical sensitivity would be consistent with the state's performance before the 1970s.[9] However, any relative reduction in the shock of the next recession due to modest debt structure could be more than offset by the demise of a significant component of enterprises still barely operating at the margin of existence.

Macroeconomic policies to promote recovery are unlikely to have any differential impact on Oklahoma. It is most unlikely that such antirecession measures will involve fiscal policy, and there is no reason to expect antirecession monetary policy to affect regions selectively.

Oklahoma and the Next Decade

Long-term predictions for economically small components of the national system are best done in a literary rather than numeric medium. With 1.3 percent of the U.S. population, Oklahoma is definitely a small component. Moreover, the energy-price-driven turbulence during 1973–86 means that recent economic trends are virtually worthless as foundations for a long-term outlook. Projections for 2000 that rely heavily on developments after 1983 will surely undershoot the mark; this period is loaded with negative one-time adjustments not to be repeated in the 1990s. However, if the frame of reference is extended backward toward the first oil-price shock in 1973, the projection will aim too high; while relative energy prices will rise in the 1990s, another tenfold increase is out of the question.

As a starting point for reviewing Oklahoma's next decade, several recent projections will be presented. These will be associated with an obligatory forecast of employment, population and income to 2000. Then the argument will be set forth that the recent history of the Oklahoma economy actually is indicative of strength rather than weakness, and thus the forecast may be on the conservative side. At the minimum, assertions that the Oklahoma economy will go nowhere in the 1990s should be rejected.

What Recent Projects Say About Oklahoma in the 1990s. The regional forecasting business is itself a growth industry. This means, presumably, that decisions, private and public, are being based partially on the data supplied. National projections by the Bureau of Labor Statistics (BLS) are an important part of the whole regional forecasting industry. Of particular interest in shaping a long-term outlook for Oklahoma is the BLS national employment projection. Table 1 contains historical data on civilian employment (household survey based) for Oklahoma and the United States, together with the BLS "moderate" projection for the United States to 2000. This national projection of 133 million does not differ greatly from those of these firms:

DRI/McGraw–Hill[10]	132.0
WEFA[11]	134.3
National Planning Association[12]	135.1

At the national level, it is reasonable to project employment as a derivative of population growth, the labor force participation rate and an average or natural rate of unemployment. However, because of the high likelihood of migration, employment becomes a determinant of population in a small, open economy, such as the Oklahoma economy. There are, of course, a few areas in the state in which migration flows and, hence, population levels are strongly influenced by the locational preferences of retirees.

The data in Table 1 suggest two propositions about Oklahoma employment growth:

- The periods 1973–84 and 1984–88 are anomalous within the context of U.S. growth and offer little insight into the future.
- The 15-year period 1958–73 was one of fairly steady but relatively slow employment growth for Oklahoma; the state's employment growth rate was 80 percent of the U.S. average.

It is reasonable to reject the 1973–88 patterns as guides for the future. Changes in demographic patterns and national economic structure in the 1990s also suggest caution in a simplistic proposition that Oklahoma's growth will bear roughly the same relation to the nation as was the case in 1958–73. Much slower national population and employment growth in the 1990s is likely to retard the neoclassical "spreading out and filling in" effects that were present in the earlier period.[13] This slow growth is particularly disturbing with respect to manufacturing. During 1958–73, national manufacturing employment grew 4.1 million;

Table 1
**Civilian Employment and Growth Rates,
Oklahoma and the United States,
Selected Years, 1958–2000**

Year	Employment (thousands)		Annual Compound Growth Rate	
	Oklahoma	United States	Oklahoma	United States
1958	846	63,036	1.6	2.0
1973	1,076	85,064	2.7	1.9
1984	1,445	105,005	–0.2	2.3
1988	1,431	114,968	?	1.2
2000	?	133,030		

Sources: Oklahoma Employment Security Commission (1989), *Handbook of Employment Statistics* Vol. I, 8f.
U.S. Department of Labor, Bureau of Labor Statistics (1988), *Projections 2000* Bulletin 2302, March, 30.
U.S. Executive Office of the President's Council of Economic Advisors (1989), *Economic Report of the President, 1989*, 344.
Monthly Labor Review, July 1989, 63.

Oklahoma picked up 1.6 percent of that growth or 67,000 manufacturing jobs. During the 1990s, U.S. manufacturing employment is unlikely to grow very much—if at all. The long-term implications of a national no-employment-growth manufacturing sector are not well-understood—especially with respect to relatively less-developed areas such as Oklahoma.

Another contrast with 1958–73 involves international debt. The Arkansas River Navigation System notwithstanding, the tremendous growth in international trade has caused fundamental changes in the pattern of locational advantage in favor of coastal regions and against land-locked states in the mid-continent, such as Oklahoma. Imports, for example, averaged only 5.5 percent of GNP during 1958–73 but stood at 12.6 percent in 1988. An import share of 15 percent by 2000 is quite reasonable.[14]

Assuming that the Oklahoma economy absorbs its current excess capacity in the early 1990s, analysts expect the state to begin to track along with the U.S. economy in a more normal fashion. At the optimistic outside, it might be assumed that the state would maintain a constant share of U.S. employment (1.244 percent in 1988). In this case, employment would increase by 224,000 by 2000. This seems overly optimistic. If, instead, the state's employment growth rate bore the same relation to national growth as during 1958–73, the employment increase would be 177,000, or an average of about 15,000 jobs per year. Although such annual increases were not unusual during 1958–73, the U.S. economy was then growing much more rapidly. Thus, a repeat of the 1958–73 growth pattern is also too much to expect. If Oklahoma employment were growing at only *half* the rate of its U.S. counterpart in the 1990s, the number of jobs would still increase by about 100,000. This is surely a safe forecast.

What sort of population change would 100,000 more jobs mean during 1988–2000? In 1988, total employment was about 44 percent of total Oklahoma population. If that ratio were maintained, state employment of, say, 1,550,000 in 2000 would imply a population of 3,522,000—up a healthy 280,000 from the 1988 level. Unfortunately for Oklahoma, an increase in the labor force participation rate, an increase in the share of the population in the 16-years-old and older (labor-force eligible) age group and a decrease in the unemployment rate may push the employment-to-population percentage upward to near the 50 percent level—implying perhaps a population *decline* of 100,000 in Oklahoma by 2000. It might, in fact, take around 175,000 more employed persons just to maintain state population at about its 1988 level (see the appendix). It should be emphasized that forecasting the various rates that determine the employment–population linkage involves a good deal of conjecture about fertility decisions, the inclination of women to seek work, the inclination of men to retire and current business-cycle conditions in 2000.

How does a negative population-growth prediction stack up against published projections? Table 2 contains projections for the state to 2000 by the U.S. Bureau of the Census, the Oklahoma Department of Commerce's Research and Planning Division and the National Planning Association. Perhaps all that Table 2 illustrates is the hazardous nature of long-term projections. None of the projections involve population decline for Oklahoma. The Census Bureau's forecast, however, is very close to no growth at all. All three projections imply that employment growth in Oklahoma during the 1990s will be much greater than the conservative forecast set forth above. Moreover, the assumption that employment determines population at the state level does not always hold; the causal relationship is clearly reversed when there is immigration of retirees.

State personal income, of course, will grow along with employment and productivity. Nationwide, forecasts for the 1990s of growth rates in total real disposable personal income are ranging between 2 percent and 2.4 percent compound. The BLS is forecasting a growth rate in real disposable per capita

Table 2
**Population Estimates and Projections for Oklahoma,
Selected Years, 1958–2000**

	U.S. Bureau of the Census	Oklahoma Department of Commerce*	National Planning Association
Historical data: (In thousands)			
1958	2,267	—	—
1973	2,694	—	—
1984	3,321	—	—
1988	3,242	—	—
Projections:			
1995	3,318	3,417	3,463
2000	3,376	3,509	3,586
Annual compound growth rate:			
1958–73	1.2	—	—
1973–84	1.9	—	—
1984–88	−0.6	—	—
1988–95	0.3	0.8	0.9
1995–2000	0.3	0.5	0.7
1988–2000	0.3	0.7	0.7

*medium series

Sources: U.S. Bureau of the Census (1988), *Projections of the Population of States by Age, Sex, and Race: 1988–2010* Series P-25, No. 1017, 20f.
Oklahoma Department of Commerce (1988), *Population Projections for Oklahoma and its Counties by Age and Sex, and for its Cities, 1980–2010*, 11.
National Planning Association, *Regional Economic Growth in the United States: Projections for 1989–2000*, Report No. 88-R-1, 53.

personal income of 1.6 percent for 1986–2000. A key question for Oklahoma is whether per capita personal income will converge toward the national level, or whether it will continue to hover around 80 percent of its national counterpart as it did in the 1950s and 1960s.

Oklahoma's per capita personal income will bear about the same relation to the U.S. figure at the end of the 1990s as at the beginning. The equilibrating forces of free markets may even cause a slight amount of convergence with the nation. But the convergence, if any, will be small in an environment in which overall state activity is growing less rapidly than that of the slow-growing nation. The best that can be said from Oklahoma's point of view is that the energy–agriculture forces leading to *divergence* of per capita income in the 1980s have largely worked themselves out. Mitigating against further convergence for states in the mid-continent area is the likely continued dominance of a "bicoastal economy" growth pattern.[15]

Recent Economic History and the Strength of the Oklahoma Economy. If the 1970s and 1980s are anomalous, then the long-term forecaster is forced into an analysis of Oklahoma's economic history in the context of strong linkages with the national economic system. The outlook for employment, population and income just presented assumes that the massive adjustment process following the energy-driven boom-bust will be essentially over by the early 1990s. It is absurd to assume that this adjustment process will continue throughout the decade. Excess capacity is working itself out through depreciation, abandonment and tenant or buyer attraction due to low rents and prices.

Two features suggest that the above forecast of 100,000 new jobs and population decline in the 1990s is quite conservative. One feature relates to long-term image, the other to strength exhibited in the midst of the post-1983 difficulties.

For reasons deeply embedded in great American fiction, Oklahoma conjures an image of population loss—of "Okies" leaving the state for a better life in California. Observers are wont to point out correctly that the state's population was less in 1960 than it had been in 1930. This observation, however, incorrectly suggests an environment of chronic economic disadvantage out-of-step with much of the rest of the nation. Certainly, there has been an increased inclination to dredge up this image since the collapse of Penn Square Bank in mid-1982. A detailed look at the annual estimates indicates that severe population decline was limited to 1935–45. In fact, state population increased relatively steadily from the end of World War II to around 1984. Net migration turned positive in the 1960s and 1970s, and with a little luck it may even remain slightly positive in the 1980s due to the burst of immigrants at the height of the oil boom.

The performance of the Oklahoma economy post-1982 is another feature suggesting underlying conditions consistent with growth during the 1990s. At first blush this may seem odd, but the argument is fairly straightforward. As bad as the numbers turned for Oklahoma in 1983–86, the really surprising feature is that they were not even worse. The reasoning is set forth using the employment-by-industry data in Table 3 and a naive economic base framework.

Table 3
Nonagricultural Wage and Salary Employment in Oklahoma—1973, 1982 and 1988
(in thousands)

	Total 1973	Change 1973–82	Total 1982	Change 1982–88	Total 1988
Total Nonagricultural Employment	851.9	365.0	1,216.9	−84.2	1,132.7
Mining	36.5	69.1	105.6	−60.7	44.9
Construction	47.4	8.3	55.7	−21.2	34.5
Manufacturing (Durables)	90.3	26.7	117.0	−15.3	101.7
Manufacturing (Nondurables)	61.7	2.0	63.7	−2.5	61.2
Transporation and Public Utilities	55.3	15.6	70.9	−8.8	62.1
Trade	196.6	92.9	289.5	−15.5	274.0
Finance, Insurance and Real Estate	42.2	18.9	61.1	−2.1	59.0
Services (Health)	45.0	24.5	69.5	7.2	76.7
Services (Other)	84.8	61.8	146.6	24.7	171.3
Government (Federal)	54.4	−5.5	48.9	.9	49.8
Government (State and Local)	137.9	50.5	188.4	9.4	197.8

Source: Oklahoma Employment Security Commission, *Oklahoma Handbook of Employment Statistics, 1988* 2:3.

There are, of course, serious deficiencies in simplistic economic base models of regional economic development with segregate sectors seen as part of an economic base or export component and a local-service component. But such an approach—treating energy, agriculture, manufacturing and federal government installations as basic—is a good starting point for viewing Oklahoma employment patterns during the energy boom from 1973 until the peak employment year of 1982. Assuming fairly stable farm employment and focusing on nonfarm establishment employment, Table 3 indicates a total employment increase of nearly four jobs for every one new job in the combined sectors of mining, manufacturing and the federal government during the expansion 1973–82. This seems to imply an employment multiplier of nearly four.

But the naive economic base model falls to pieces during the energy-driven bust between 1982 and 1988. During this contraction, the total decline in employment was nearly equal to the decline in these basic sectors. (The total decline exceeded the decline in these basic sectors by only 8.5 percent.) Ignoring a somewhat shorter response time, the total nonfarm payroll employment decline would have been roughly four times greater had Oklahoma's bust been structurally symmetrical to its boom with respect to these basic sectors.

Why this lack of symmetry in the boom and bust periods? Several features appear to have been operating.

- Very strong national employment growth after 1982 affected Oklahoma's employment pattern; from 1982 through 1988, national nonfarm payroll employment grew at an annual rate of 2.8 percent.
- The state's underlying long-term growth was based largely on conditions other than oil and gas during the 1950s and 1960s; from 1950 through 1973, state total employment grew at a 2.6-percent annual rate. Some of the structural features creating this growth, such as location and low relative energy costs, continued to have a positive growth impact during the post-1982 recession.
- Without a series of major state tax increases in 1985–87, state and local governments (especially school districts) would have had to implement significant cutbacks; instead, state and local government employment grew by 9,400 during 1982–88.
- Several major sectors of the state's economy exhibited a reduction in the average work week between 1982 and 1988; if retail trade (except eating and drinking establishments) had not cut the average work week from 34.3 hours to 31.1 hours between 1982 and 1988, employment would have dropped by an additional 13,400.
- Personal income not directly associated with working (rent, interest and dividends and transfer payments) exhibited an expanded share of

Oklahoma's total personal income during the difficult times between 1982 and 1988. A major portion of this type of income entered the state's general flow of spending largely through the initial purchase of consumer goods and services.

- The portion of the state's manufacturing sector producing inputs for the oil and gas sector proved more viable than might have been expected; although many establishments shut down or cut back, there was also a good deal of adjusting product lines to other markets. As of August 1989, more than 7,000 workers in the state were still producing oil field machinery—with heavy emphasis on world markets.
- Oklahoma's service-sector employment grew 14.8 percent during 1982–88. This was only half the rate of service employment growth nationally, but this suggests that services have an economic life of their own. There clearly is an important export base component within Oklahoma's services sector.

Embedded in this failure to collapse even further in the 1980s are sources of strength likely to work to the state's advantage during the 1990s. Except for the reduction of the average work week, which spread the wage bill across more workers, all the points listed above will have a positive effect on Oklahoma's growth during the 1990s. The national economy, although growing more slowly than in recent decades, will continue to provide expanding markets for state goods and services. International markets will become more important. There are strong signs that the state and local government sector will continue to be an important source of employment growth as greater emphasis is placed on education and possibly on more vigorous infrastructure replacement and construction. Even transfers and the rent–interest–dividends source of household spending will grow as eastern and southern Oklahoma attract retirees. With real oil prices rising perhaps 25 percent by the turn of the century, even the components of the state's manufacturing sector specializing in inputs for oil and gas production will improve. Health services and business services will continue to be important growth-generators in the 1990s.

Conclusion with Downside Risks

The predictions of no recession in 1990, greater resilience in the next recession (whenever that may be) and modest but substantial growth in employment in the 1990s are not likely to stimulate a flow of Sooner adrenalin—especially when the employment growth is not sufficient to prevent population decline. Lest this be viewed as an unreasonably pessimistic scenario, it is worth concluding with comments on downside risks largely related to the expectation that the 1990s will be truly a "different decade."

Despite the failure of the 1987 crash to have a perceptible impact on the macroeconomy, stock market instability in the autumn of 1989 is a reminder that the soft landing could turn rough very quickly. A recession in 1990 would create more severe stress on Oklahoma than one that might occur mid-decade.

But what about the next decade? A small economy like Oklahoma's can be buffeted by events external and internal that would barely be noticed in a big economy like that of Texas. Very successful efforts at stimulating manufacturing can be wiped out in one or two fell swoops by events at big plants. The recent dramatic growth of Japanese auto manufacturing capacity in North America will threaten the viability of virtually all domestic facilities during the next decade— including General Motors' giant Oklahoma City facility. To date, GM, with 20 percent excess vehicle capacity, has not announced plans for its Oklahoma operation once it phases out its A-body cars.[16] Moreover, the structure of much manufacturing in the state renders it sensitive to exchange-rate fluctuations and cost of production conditions abroad. A particularly ominous note was the September 1989 announcement by AT&T Technologies Inc. that it was shifting its Oklahoma City cable-making operations to Monterrey, Mexico.[17] Big, single-facility changes can make quantum differences in other sectors, too. Consider this: The recent closing of Oral Roberts' City of Faith complex in Tulsa increased by 20 percent the city's already bloated stock of vacant office space.[18]

Other sources of downside risk are related to the public sector. At the state and local government levels, it is now settled that states and communities that offer superior educational systems and that have not allowed their public infrastructure to deteriorate will capture a disproportionate share of national economic growth in the 1990s. On the eve of the new decade, the verdict is still out as to whether Oklahoma will implement massive improvement in its now substandard systems of elementary, secondary and higher education. So, too, is the verdict still out on infrastructure. It may, in fact, prove impossible for a state accustomed to taxing itself relatively lightly—and with per capita income only four-fifths that of the U.S. average—to deal adequately with *either* education or infrastructure, let alone both at the same time.

Federal government policy also involves some downside risk in the 1990s. Oklahoma's military installations at Lawton, Altus, Enid, McAlester and Midwest City are an important part of the state's economic base. A different, more peaceful, decade in international relations could mean fundamental shifts in defense policy by 2000. These shifts are likely to mean fewer facilities of smaller scale than is the case today. Oklahoma's small towns and rural areas have already felt the effect of reduced federal government involvement in regional development during the 1980s. Although emphasis on rural development is growing in Washington, D.C., effective policies not involving major federal funding are difficult to sort out. There is also potential trouble on the farm policy front if the 1990s bring a strong drift toward "decoupling" financial support to needy farmers from commodity programs.

The downside risks for Oklahoma interact with the prospects for slow growth in the 1990s to create an overall economic environment that is relatively risky. There is an old adage that "Oklahoma is a capital-short state." Yet even the most casual glance at loan-to-deposit ratios and federal funds flowing from state commercial banks partially belies this conventional wisdom of capital shortage. When it comes to capital markets in Oklahoma, there are some problems on the demand side as well as on the supply side—problems linked to regional risk. Just as sure as economic growth will return to Oklahoma in the 1990s, so will that growth sometimes involve greater risk than in the more favored parts of the nation. The ultimate questions are: How big is that risk, how frequently will it be encountered, and how difficult will it be to overcome? That is what makes the 1990s an especially different decade for Oklahoma.

Notes

[1] *Oklahoma Department of Commerce 1989.*

[2] *Oklahoma State University 1989.*

[3] *The WEFA Group 1989b.*

[4] *Southwestern Bell Telephone Company 1989.*

[5] *State of Oklahoma 1989.*

[6] Journal Record *1989.*

[7] *Oklahoma Department of Commerce 1989.*

[8] Tulsa World *1989.*

[9] *Bretzfelder 1973.*

[10] *DRI/McGraw–Hill 1989, A76.*

[11] *WEFA 1989, 1.7.*

[12] *National Planning Association 1989, 4.*

[13] *Perloff 1960.*

[14] *DRI/McGraw–Hill 1989.*

[15] *Coughlin and Madelbaum 1988.*

[16] Wall Street Journal *1989.*

[17] Journal Record *1989b.*

[18] Tulsa World *1989b.*

Appendix

A Note on the Relationship Between Employment and Population

By definition, three variables affect the link between employment and population. These are (1) the percentage of the total population 16 years old and older, (2) the labor force participation rate and (3) the unemployment rate. The variables are linked in the following manner:

$$\text{Population} = \frac{\text{Employment}}{\begin{array}{ccc} \text{Percent 16} & \text{Labor force} & \text{1–Unemployment} \\ \text{and over} & \text{participation} & \text{rate} \\ & \text{rate} & \end{array}}$$

In 1986, for example, about 75.9 percent of Oklahoma's population was 16 years old and older, the labor force participation rate was 64 percent, and the unemployment rate was 8.2 percent. Using the above formula, an estimated state population of 3,305,000 is consistent with the estimated employment level of 1,473,000.

The Bureau of the Census projects Oklahoma's 16-years-old and older group to be 78.3 percent of the state's total population in 2000.[1] The Bureau of Labor Statistics projects a national labor force participation rate for 2000 that is 2.5 percentage points above its 1986 level.[2] Using these two relationships, and assuming an Oklahoma unemployment rate of 5 percent and employment of 1.55 million in 2000, leads to the following results:

$$3{,}134 = \frac{1{,}550}{(.783)\ \ (.665)\ \ (1-.05)}$$

Specifically, this exercise indicates an increase in Oklahoma employment of 77,000 between 1986 and 2000 (or 119,000 between 1988 and 2000), which is consistent with a population decline of 171,000 (or 108,000 between 1988 and 2000).

[1]*U.S. Bureau of the Census 1988.*
[2]*U.S. Bureau of Labor Statistics 1988, 23.*

References

Bretzfelder, Robert B. (1972), "Sensitivity of State and Regional Income to National Business Cycles," *Survey of Current Business*, April, 22–27.

Coughlin, Cletus C., and Thomas B. Madelbaum (1988), "Why Have State Per Capita Incomes Diverged Recently?" Federal Reserve Bank of St. Louis *Review*, October, 24–36.

DRI/McGraw–Hill (1989), *U.S. Long-Term Review* (Lexington, Mass.: Standard and Poor's Corporation, Summer).

Journal Record (Oklahoma City) (1989a), "State Economy Situated for Slow Growth," July 12, 1.

———— (1989b), "AT&T Cable Production to Leave OKC for Mexico," Sept. 23, 1.

National Planning Association (1987), *Prospects for U.S. Economic Growth, 1988–2010* (Washington, D.C.: NPA Data Services, 87-N-1).

Oklahoma Department of Commerce (1989), "October Indicators," news release, Oct. 11.

Oklahoma State University (1989), *Oklahoma Quarterly Economic Forecast* (Stillwater, Okla.: Oklahoma State University, Office of Business and Economic Research, July).

Perloff, Harvey S., *et al* (1960), *Regions, Resources, and Economic Growth* (Lincoln, Neb.: University of Nebraska Press).

Southwestern Bell Telephone Company (1989), *The General Business Index, and Analysis of Oklahoma's Economy*, Oklahoma City, Sept. 28.

State of Oklahoma, Office of State Finance (1989), *Oklahoma Revenue* 90-2, Sept. 30.

Tulsa World (1989a), "Price of State Crude Expected to Tumble," Oct. 11, B2.

———— (1989b), "Realtor Views City of Faith as Local Asset," Oct. 12, B1.

U.S. Bureau of the Census (1988), *Projections of the Population of States by Age, Sex, and Race: 1988–2010*, Series P-25, No. 1017.

U.S. Bureau of Labor Statistics (1988), *Projections 2000*, Bulletin 2302, March.

Wall Street Journal (1989), "GM Indicates Glum Tidings for 5 Facilities," Oct. 16, A3.

The WEFA Group (1989a), *U.S. Long-Term Economic Outllook* Vol. 1, *Trend/ Moderate Growth Scenario* (Bala Cynwyd, Penn.: The WEFA Group, first quarter).

—— (1989b), "Regional Outlook: Will the Rebound Continue?" Presentation at Oklahoma City, Okla., Sept. 14.

Regional Economic Cycles and the Texas Economy

Barton A. Smith

M ost analyses of regional economies are based on some form of an export base model driven by exogenous factors determined outside the region. Typically, empirical versions are driven by national economic projections from large-scale and well-known macroeconomic models, such as those maintained by the Wharton School of Business at the University of Pennsylvania or by Data Resources Inc. in Washington, D.C. The problem is that the link between the national economy and regional economies can become very difficult to isolate. Often, the ups and downs of a regional economy do not coincide with other regions' or with the national economy's.

To better understand regional economic fluctuations, it is useful to distinguish between different types of regional cycles. The simplest dichotomy is between fluctuations in a region's economic base and fluctuations in its secondary sectors. The simple multiplier effect of export base models suggests that there should be a direct correlation between base and secondary activity, but in reality that relationship is quite complex. This is especially true for capital-producing secondary sectors, such as construction, that are vulnerable to accelerator cycles that involve extremely large swings in activity and employment. Because this phenomenon primarily involves the regional real estate market, I refer to these cycles as *regional real estate cycles*.

Real estate cycles are based on adjustments in the stock demand and supply of housing and commercial real estate. They often occur simply because of accumulated overbuilding. Thus, regions can experience rather substantial declines in construction activity and employment even if the region's economic base continues to grow.

Fluctuations in a region's economic base can also be divided into two types: those that are directly tied to macroeconomic fluctuations in the national economy and those that are tied to variations in demand for the region's economic base, independent of macroeconomic influences. The ups and downs of the automobile industry in Detroit serve as an example of a *nationally driven economic base cycle.* The behavior of energy-driven economies during the 1970s and 1980s illustrates *counter-cyclical economic base cycles.*

The Texas economy has been a regional economist's nightmare. The national recessions of 1974–75 and 1982 are barely visible in Texas statistics. Indeed, during those national recessions, the Texas economy was going in the opposite direction. In part, this was because what was good for the oil patch, namely higher oil prices, was detrimental to the nation. In part, the counter-cyclical timing was merely coincidental.

The counter-cyclical nature of the Texas economy gave the illusion that Texas was recession-proof. In 1981, as the national economy rapidly slid into the worst national recession since the Great Depression, Texas experienced record growth. However, beginning in 1983 the national economy embarked upon recovery and expansion of impressive strength and duration, while in Texas much of the rest of the decade was an economic disaster (Chart 1).

The Heterogeneity of the Texas Economy

Analyses of the aggregate economic statistics for Texas can be quite misleading. In fact, it may be a mistake to talk about the "Texas economy." Texas

Chart 1
Annual Employment Growth Rates,
Nonagricultural Wage and Salary Employment

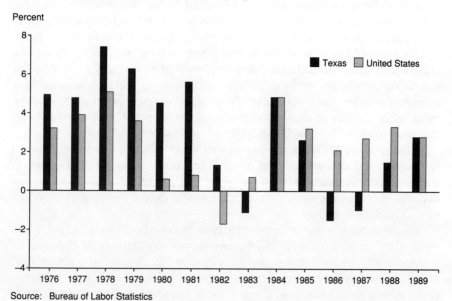

Source: Bureau of Labor Statistics

is not only big, it is also highly diverse. What drives the Dallas economy is different from what drives the Houston economy or the Valley economy or the West Texas economy. These relatively independent economic regions need not be in sync. These diverse regions can experience economic cycles for different reasons and with different timing.

Commentators frequently refer to the Texas recession and presume that all of the state's woes had the same roots—the oil bust of the mid-1980s. Several things appeared to link the entire state together: the slump in real estate markets, the failure of banks and the timing of these problems coincident with the plunge in oil prices in 1986. Yet, more careful observation reveals very different forces acting within Texas' many economic regions.

The Early 1980s. Differences in the Texas economies became evident in the early 1980s as the national economic slowdown clearly influenced the Dallas and San Antonio regions. Both areas, however, avoided significant job losses. Houston's economy, on the other hand, soared. On the surface, 1981 seemed to set the stage for another decade of unprecedented growth.

Beginning in 1983, San Antonio, Austin and Dallas embarked on a growth spree driven by the national recovery and a local construction boom (Charts 2

Chart 2
San Antonio and Texas Employment Indexes,
Nonagricultural Wage and Salary

Employment index

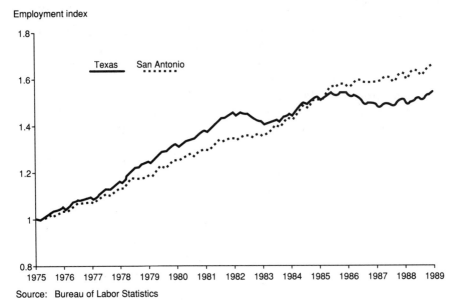

Source: Bureau of Labor Statistics

Chart 3
Dallas and Texas Employment Indexes,
Nonagricultural Wage and Salary

Employment index

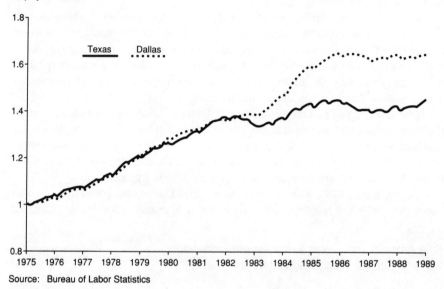

Source: Bureau of Labor Statistics

and 3). In contrast, by the end of 1983 Houston had lost more than 150,000 jobs, mostly because of enormous layoffs by firms manufacturing oil field equipment (Chart 4). Had it not been for Houston, Midland–Odessa and Beaumont, Texas would have had banner years in the mid-1980s.

The Bottom Falls Out in 1986. Almost everywhere in Texas, 1986 was a bummer, but a closer examination reveals that the reasons for the bad economic environment were quite diverse. Growth of U.S. industrial production virtually halted, and the impact rippled through Texas manufacturing as well. This slowdown hurt nonenergy manufacturing in Dallas and downstream energy manufacturing (refining and petrochemicals) in Houston and Beaumont.

Falling oil prices in 1986 resulted in another wave of layoffs in upstream energy employment in Houston, but together with the falling dollar, the falling prices provided the foundation for a remarkable resurgence in downstream energy activity beginning in 1987. Perhaps the most significant feature of 1986 was that the impact of overbuilding spread to Austin, San Antonio and Dallas. Despite stable or growing economic bases, all three regions experienced major contractions in construction activity and employment.

The Start of a Turnaround. Beginning in early 1987, the Houston economy began to show definite signs of life, and since then it has added more than 100,000 jobs to regional payrolls. Meanwhile, the Dallas economy continued to struggle through two more years of stagnation. But this struggle was not because the Dallas economy was weaker than the Houston economy. The two economies simply were experiencing rather different cycles.

Houston experienced a severe counter-cyclical base contraction and a major real estate downturn. Before it was over, Houston's employment fell by more than 200,000 jobs from its April 1982 peak.

Dallas, however, just stopped growing. Actual job loss was minimal. The Dallas slowdown was primarily related to a real-estate-driven construction cycle. There was no significant loss in the economic base; the slowdown was merely the natural consequence of too much building activity in the early 1980s. Unlike the Houston recession that began in early 1982, the Dallas slowdown did not begin until 1986. While the Houston economy was establishing a bottom to its recession that year, the Dallas economy was just beginning to respond to the weight of excess commercial and residential real estate.

Chart 4
Houston and Texas Employment Indexes,
Nonagricultural Wage and Salary

Employment index

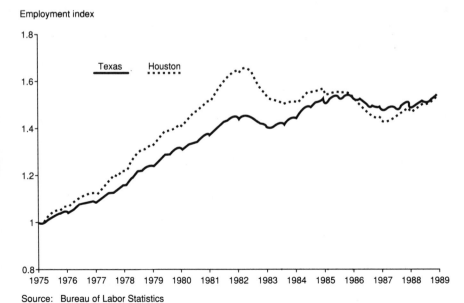

Source: Bureau of Labor Statistics

Understanding the Oil Boom and Bust

As we look to the future, it is useful to reexamine the role energy has played in many of the state's regions. A four-decade perspective clearly reveals that the oil boom between 1973 and 1981 was an aberration. Surprisingly, economic growth in Texas continued strong throughout the 1950s and 1960s despite moderately falling real dollar prices for crude and sharply falling rig counts (Chart 5). During those decades, the energy economy was more evenly balanced between upstream (exploration) and downstream (the production of final energy products). The energy economy was relatively healthy in 1970 with prices less than $3 per barrel and the rig count hovering around 1,000 rigs.

The sharp rise in oil prices in 1973–74 dramatically altered the energy industry for a decade. The impact of the price spike then and again in 1979–80 was almost exclusively focused on upstream energy sectors. The manufacture of oil field equipment increased fourfold, and mining employment more than doubled. Suddenly, searching for oil in the most inhospitable places became economically feasible, and Texas was at the forefront of the search. Not since the turn of the century, with the discovery of Spindletop and subsequent fields,

Chart 5
Real Price of Oil and Rig Count;
Posted Price, West Texas Intermediate Crude Oil (in 1988 dollars)

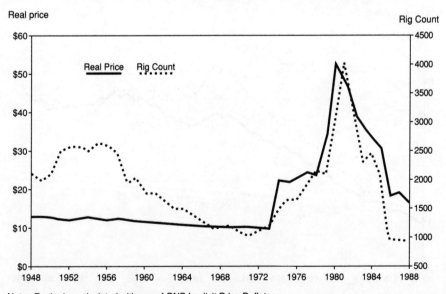

Note: Real price calculated with use of GNP Implicit Price Deflator

Chart 6
Oil Rigs Available vs. Rigs Active

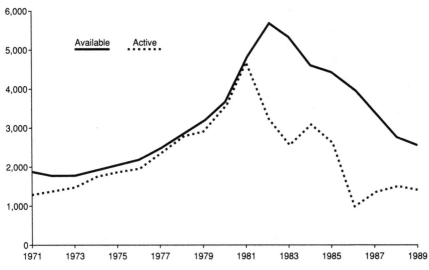

Source: Reed Tool Company

had upstream activity so dominated economic growth. Approximately 85 percent of all economic growth in Houston between 1973 and 1981 was directly related to exploration.

Because this growth primarily involved the production of producer durables (oil field equipment), this part of the Texas economy became very susceptible to severe accelerator swings. (For more details on the accelerator effect, see *The Handbook on the Houston Economy*, 1986 edition, University of Houston Center for Public Policy.) Thus, just when everyone began to think Texas was recession-proof, the structure of the energy economy was becoming progressively vulnerable to a sudden reversal.

The typical accelerator cycle does not require much of an exogenous shock to create a sharp contraction in employment in the capital-producing sectors. During 1981 and 1982, the price of oil fell by only a few dollars per barrel. This small decline was sufficient to reduce the utilized rig count from more than 4,000 to less than 2,500 (Chart 6). With the market swamped with excess equipment, new production was totally unnecessary. Thus, a $3 drop in the price of oil resulted in a 40-percent drop in exploration, which, in turn, resulted in almost a 100-percent drop in the production of oil filed capital equipment.

Oil prices did not really collapse until 1986, but by then most of the damage had already been done. By the end of that year, most of the gains that occurred between 1973 and 1981 had vanished. After the dust settled, the energy economy in 1987 looked much more like the energy economy of the late 1960s.

Oil price changes still influence the Texas economy, but while oil prices have now risen 100 percent from those 1986 lows, upstream energy has shown little life because excess supplies of oil field equipment remain. Once the market absorbs those excesses, rising oil prices will once again stimulate upstream energy in Texas.

Actually, this aspect of the state's energy future is encouraging. The gap between stock demand and stock supply of oil field equipment has been steadily closing since 1987. At the current pace, most excesses will be eliminated by 1992. Thus, even if the rig count remains at current levels, some life should return to the upstream portion of Texas' energy economy within two or three years.

However, other changes since the boom suggest that Texas' energy economy will never be the same. At the beginning of the boom, worldwide exploration expertise and equipment-production capacity was concentrated in the United States in general, and Texas in particular. But the tenfold increase in oil prices created the economic resources and incentives to develop exploration capabilities worldwide. In the future, Texas producers of oil field equipment will face stiff foreign competition.

Perhaps an even more important change is that the United States and Texas are running out of easily accessible oil. Despite the sharp price increases during the 1970s, Texas production of crude continued to fall, and this decline will continue (Chart 7). Such a decline not only has important implications for state revenues, but it also means that Texas refineries will become progressively dependent on imported crude and that exploration will focus on more promising foreign discoveries. With relatively high labor costs added to the transportation costs of delivery abroad, Texas producers of oil field equipment will find it in-

Chart 7
Taxable Crude Oil Production in Texas

Barrels (millions)

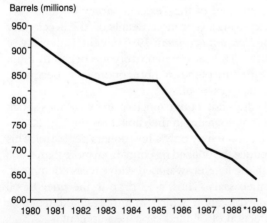

* Forecast
Source: Texas Comptroller of Public Accounts

creasingly difficult to compete. The industry's primary hope is to maintain the technological edge required to keep a foothold in the foreign exploration effort.

It will be some time before the real dollar price of oil returns to its 1980 high. Currently, levels of excess capacity in the international oil market exceed 10 million barrels per day (Chart 8). Recent increases in world demand are encouraging, but at the current pace the demand for crude will still take much of this decade to catch up with world production capacity. Furthermore, in response to falling prices, exploratory industries are rapidly finding cheaper ways to explore for oil. Prices more than $24 per barrel would almost certainly accelerate the search for oil worldwide, expanding capacity even more.

This does not mean the prices will not rise. Today's price of $22 per barrel is equivalent to only $13 per barrel in terms of 1980 dollars. The current economics of the international oil market suggests, however, that it will be a long time before we see real dollar prices back to $36 per barrel.

Distinguishing the Separate Effects of Real Estate Cycles

One widely accepted myth is that the real estate debacle in Texas was generated by the slump in the energy sector. This notion is even carried to the

Chart 8
World Oil Capacity and Consumption

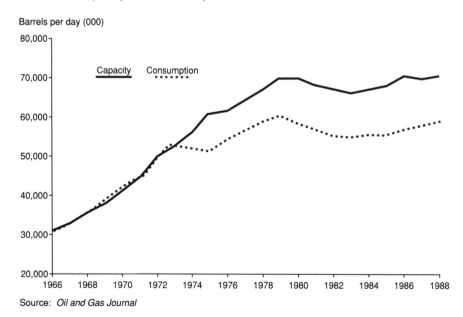

Barrels per day (000)

Source: *Oil and Gas Journal*

extreme by some observers who think that the price of Texas real estate is directly tied to the price of oil. This, however, is far from the truth.

Real estate cycles are common to all regions of the United States, although they are more prevalent in growing areas. Real estate cycles can occur in the absence of any significant economic slowdown within the rest of a regional economy. These cycles are often precipitated by changes in an area's growth rate. If a region has been growing at a 4-percent pace, builders and developers tend to expect that rate to persist, and they build accordingly. If the region slows to a 2-percent growth rate, which is still quite healthy, overbuilding will occur, nonetheless. Overbuilding then sets the stage for a buildup of excess inventories of vacant real estate, downward pressures on rents and prices, and a significant contraction of building activity and employment during subsequent years.

New York and Atlanta were noted for soft real estate markets in the early 1970s. Cities in Arizona and Florida are just beginning to struggle with serious excess supply problems. In fact, Phoenix has gone through at least three real estate cycles in the past two decades.

Overbuilding may have been somewhat worse in Texas because the state lacks constraints, making entry into the industry quite easy. The advantage of unrestricted building was that costs were surprisingly contained, even during the boom years of the 1970s. The disadvantage was that individual builders failed to see the marketwide excesses until it was too late.

In 1982 and 1983, builders in Houston established new construction records, adding approximately 125,000 housing units to the existing stock (Chart 9). Houston's buildup coincided with the loss of 160,000 jobs in the local economy and a decline in the metropolitan population of almost 30,000 residents. No doubt, oil patch woes magnified the problems. Even so, had Houston continued to grow as it did during the 1970s, the construction industry still built at least 50,000 housing units more than could possibly have been absorbed. In other words, even if oil prices and rig counts had not slumped, the Houston real estate market would have still experienced a significant correction.

That is what happened in Dallas, Austin and San Antonio. None of these communities felt the brunt of the energy recession. The economic bases of these communities never declined. Nonetheless, all of these cities were grossly overbuilt. The impact of the energy recession on Houston initiated that city's real estate cycle three years earlier than in other cities. Without the recession, Houston would have joined the rest of Texas in the broader statewide real estate bust that began in 1986.

The problem was simply overbuilding. The solution was to stop building and then to wait. The cure takes time. Excesses must be absorbed by eventual economic growth and by the retirement of the obsolete portions of the existing stock.

Houston was the first city to take the cure; construction started to fall in 1982. Dallas and San Antonio, on the other hand, did not experience significant declines in construction until 1986 (Charts 10 and 11). Despite more severe economic reversal, Houston's excesses were not much greater than excesses elsewhere in the state. Vacancy rates for residential and commercial properties were very similar throughout much of the state. Thus, one can expect similar lapse-time requirements. In Houston, the real estate market bottomed in 1987; in Dallas and San Antonio, the market bottomed in 1989. These markets took about five years to establish a bottom and will take another five years to absorb the remaining inventory.

The impact of this recent real estate cycle in Texas was unusual in that it generated vacancy rates and price declines substantially above levels typical of ordinary cycles. The severity was such that it brought down much of Texas' financial industry with it. However, the employment declines that amounted to approximately a 50-percent reduction in all cities were quite typical. During the mid-1990s, one source of employment growth will be construction industries, as this part of the Texas economy gradually returns to normal.

Chart 9
Houston and Texas Employment Indexes—Construction

Employment index

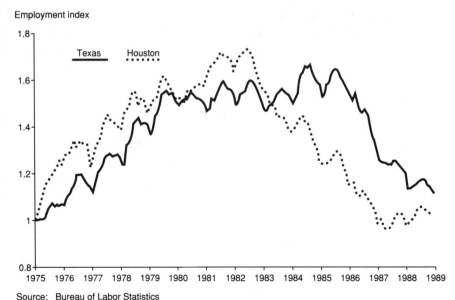

Source: Bureau of Labor Statistics

Chart 10
Dallas and Texas Employment Indexes—Construction

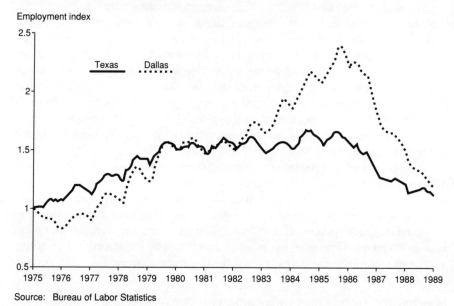

Employment index

Texas   Dallas

Source: Bureau of Labor Statistics

The Business Cycle and Prices

Most regional business cycles generate price effects that tend to stabilize the ups and downs. During booms, relative prices compared to those in other regions begin to creep upward, gradually altering the comparative advantage of one region over another. During regional recessions, low prices and wages set the stage for recovery, attracting new capital and economic development. Today, with so much of American industry being footloose, this process is even more powerful.

In 1970, Houston had the lowest cost of living of any major city in the United States. This was an important attraction to capital and labor. During the boom years, Houston had the highest inflation rate in the United States, with cost of living above the national average for the first time since the statistics have been kept. The deflation of the mid-1980s reversed those inflationary years of the 1970s, and Houston returned as the lowest-cost major city in the United States.

To a large extent, the current monetary advantage drives today's economic growth. All the major cities in Texas are a bargain, inducing firm relocation and expansion and attracting labor. Low living costs translate into low nominal wages, which provide Texas industry with a significant competitive edge.

This boon to economic development will not last forever. As recovery continues and employment growth results in the elimination of excesses in both labor and capital markets, prices will once again return to normal levels, This process should be complete by the mid-1990s. By then, economic development must proceed on a more permanent basis.

The Long-Run Prospects

Because U.S. industry is more footloose than ever, regional economic development is becoming progressively more dependent on the amenity package that a community offers. While amenities may include fiscal considerations, such as business and personal taxes, they also include the adequate provision of services. Surveys of businesses that have relocated often cite public education, local services and quality of life as dominant considerations in their site selection. Large urban areas that become overwhelmed by problems clearly repel economic development. Development restrictions that are too onerous repel new capital, as do chaotic planning and environment degradation. The key to an economic development strategy is to find the right balance between development and quality of life. While each region has its own set of natural amenities, wise economic planning will seek to appropriately exploit those

Chart 11
San Antonio and Texas Employment Indexes—Construction

Employment index

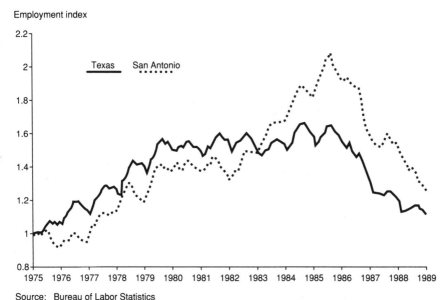

Source: Bureau of Labor Statistics

advantages to the fullest.

As Texas prepares for the 21st century, it would do well to recognize some basic changes from the past few decades that will make the new century significantly different from the past and that will influence the state's direction and potential. First, oil will play a much different role in Texas during the next century. In the very short run, the energy economy will remain relatively subdued. Substantial excess productive capacity in international oil markets still exists, and it should keep a lid on oil prices for a few more years. Excess inventories of oil field equipment also persist, but these inventories are being worked off. By 1992, a modest recovery should occur in energy-related manufacturing. However, do not expect the manufacturing of oil field equipment to return to its former glory soon, if ever. Even when worldwide exploration ascends to new heights, U.S. and Texas production of oil field equipment will not likely return to its peak levels of 1981.

In the longer run, the most ominous cloud on the horizon is the prospect of continuing declines in statewide production of crude. It is virtually certain that production levels will not return to their previous highs.

This, of course, has fiscal implications for the state. In addition, exploration activity will be much farther removed from Texas' exploration industries. Whether places like Houston can continue as international centers for world-wide exploration that will be concentrated abroad depends on whether their industries can maintain technological advantages to outweigh production and transportation cost disadvantages.

The Texas economy should diversify away from energy in terms of its share of gross regional product during the next few decades. Thus, for Texas to enjoy the same growth that it experienced during the past three decades, it must compete in terms other than proximity to natural resources. Challenges must be successfully met in the areas of educating a bilingual population; ameliorating urban problems of congestion, mobility and crime; stimulating technological innovation; protecting the environment and efficiently providing government services.

Projecting economic activity in the short run is relatively simple right now. Texas is clearly in the recovery stage of a regional economic cycle. Projecting economic activity in the long run is much more difficult because not only are there more unknowns in the distant future, but also because those unknowns largely depend on community decisions that we are just now beginning to face. While every region has certain naturally endowed advantages that influence economic growth and wealth, the economic health of most regions and countries depends largely on the social and institutional decisions and structure that allow economic development to thrive.